C HEIKH HAMIDOU KANE was born in 1928 in Mataru in Senegal. Having started at a Koranic school he eventually went to read philosophy and law at the University of Paris before training as an administrator at the Ecole Nationale de la France d'Outre-Mer. He returned to Senegal in 1959 and has become in turn the Director of the Department of Economic Planning and Development, Governor of the Region of Thiès and Commissioner of Planning in Mamadou Dia's government. More recently he has worked for UNICEF in Lagos and Abidjan. *L'Aventure Ambique* was published by Juillard in 1961 and won the 1962 Grand Prix Littéraire de l'Afrique Noir.

AMBIGUOUS ADVENTURE

AMBIGUOUS ADVENTURE

CHEIKH HAMIDOU KANE

Translated from the French
by Katherine Woods

HEINEMANN

Heinemann is an imprint of Pearson Education Limited,
a company incorporated in England and Wales, having its
registered office at Edinburgh Gate, Harlow, Essex, CM20 2JE.
Registered company number: 872828

Heinemann Publishers (Pty) Limited

PO Box 781940, Sandton 2146, Johannesburg, South Africa

OXFORD   MELBOURNE   AUCKLAND
JOHANNESBURG BLANTYRE   GABORONE
IBADAN   PORTSMOUTH (NH) USA   CHICAGO

First published in France as
L'aventure ambique
© 1962 by René Julliard
Copyright © this translation 1963 by
Walker and Company, New York, a division
of Publications Development Corporation, U.S.A.
First published in the *African Writers Series* 1972

AFRICAN WRITERS SERIES and CARIBBEAN WRITERS SERIES
and their accompanying logos are trademarks in the
United States of America of Heinemann:
A Division of Pearson Education Limited

ISBN: 978 0 435901 19 6

Printed and bound in Great Britain by
Cox & Wyman Ltd, Reading, Berkshire

08   27

PART ONE

That day, Thierno had beaten him again. And yet Samba Diallo knew his sacred verse.

It was only that he had made a slip of the tongue. Thierno had jumped up as if he had stepped on one of the white-hot paving stones of the gehenna promised to evil-doers. He had seized Samba Diallo by the fleshy part of his thigh and, between his thumb and index finger, had given him a long hard pinch. The child had gasped with pain and begun to shake all over. Threatened by sobs which were strangling him in the chest and throat, he had had the strength to master his suffering; in a weak voice, broken and stammering, but correctly, he had repeated the verse from the holy Book which he had spoken badly in the first place. The teacher's rage rose by one degree.

"Ah! So you can keep from making mistakes? Then why do you make them? Eh? Why?"

The teacher had let go of Samba Diallo's thigh. Now he was holding him by the ear and, cutting through the cartilage of the lobe, his nails met. Although the little boy had often submitted to this punishment, he could not hold back a slight groan.

"Repeat it! Again! Again!"

The teacher had shifted the grip of his fingernails, and they were now piercing the cartilage at another place. The child's ear, already white with scarcely healed scars, was bleeding anew. Samba Diallo's whole body was trembling, and he was trying his hardest to recite his verse correctly, and to restrain the whimpering that pain was wresting from him.

"Be accurate in repeating the Word of your Lord. He has done you the gracious favor of bringing His own speech down to you. These words have been veritably pronounced by the Master of the World. And you, miserable lump of earthly mold that you are, when you have the honor of repeating them after Him, you go so far as to profane them by your carelessness. You deserve to have your tongue cut a thousand times . . ."

"Yes, master . . . I ask your pardon . . . I will not make a mistake again. Listen . . ."

Once more, trembling and gasping, he repeated the flashing sentence. His eyes were imploring, his voice was fading away, his little body was burning with fever, his heart was beating wildly. This sentence—which he did not understand, for which he was suffering martyrdom—he loved for its mystery and its somber beauty. This word was not like other words. It was a word which demanded suffering, it was a word come from God, it was a miracle, it was as God Himself had uttered it. The teacher was right. The Word which comes from God must be spoken exactly as it has pleased Him to fashion it. Whoever defaces it deserves to die.

The child succeeded in mastering his suffering, completely. He repeated the sentence without stumbling, calmly, steadily, as if his body were not throbbing with pain.

The teacher released the bleeding ear. Not one tear had coursed down the child's delicate face. His voice was tranquil and his delivery restrained. The Word of God flowed pure and limpid from his fervent lips. There was a murmur in his aching head. He contained within himself the totality of the world, the visible and the invisible, its past and its future. This word which he was bringing forth in pain was the architecture of the world—it was the world itself.

The teacher, who was now holding a burning faggot from the hearth very close to the child, was looking at him and listening to him. But while his hand was threatening, his eager gaze was full of admiration, and his attention drank in the words the little boy spoke. What purity! What a miracle! Truly, this child was a gift from God. In the forty years that he had devoted himself to the task—and how meritorious a task it was!—of opening to God the intelligence of the sons of men, the teacher had never encountered anyone who, as much as this child, and in all facets of his character, waited on God with such a spirit. So closely would he live with God, this child, and the man he would become, that he could aspire—the teacher was convinced of this—to the most exalted levels of human grandeur. Yet, conversely, the least eclipse—but God forbid! The teacher was driving this eventuality from his mind with all the force of his faith. Still looking closely at the child, he made, mentally, a short prayer: "Lord, never forsake the man that is awaking in this child. May the smallest measure of Thy sovereign authority not leave him, for the smallest instant of time . . ."

As he intoned the sacred text the little boy was thinking, "Lord, Thy word must be pronounced as Thou hast spoken it . . ."

The blazing faggot was scorching his skin. He jumped up, gave a spasmodic shake to the light shirt he was wearing, and sat down again, his legs crossed, his eyes lowered to his writing-tablet, some steps away from the teacher. He took up his verse once more, and rectified his error.

"Here, come close! When vain thoughts distract you from the Word, I shall burn you . . . Pay attention: you can do that. Repeat with me, 'God, give me attentiveness.' "

"God, give me attentiveness."

"Again."

"God, give me attentiveness."

"Now go back to your verse."

Trembling and submissive, the child took up the impassioned intoning of the incandescent text. He repeated the verse over and over until he was close to losing consciousness.

The teacher, his equanimity restored, had plunged into prayer. The child knew his lesson for the morning.

At a sign from the teacher, the boy had put away his writing-tablet. But he did not move from where he was sitting. He was engrossed in a scrutiny of his schoolmaster, whom he now saw in profile. The man was old, emaciated, withered and shrunken by mortifications of the flesh. He used never to laugh. The

only moments of enthusiasm that could be seen in him
were those in which, lost in his mystic meditations or
listening to the recital of the Word of God, he would
stand erect, all tense, and seem to be lifted from the
earth, as if raised by some inner force. There were
many times, on the other hand, when, driven to a frenzied rage by the laziness or the blunders of one of his
pupils, he would give himself up to outrageously brutal
outbreaks of violence. But these outbreaks of violence
were factors in, expressions of, the interest he took in
the disciple who was at fault. The more he held him in
esteem, the wilder were his rages. Then switches, burning faggots, anything that might come to hand would
serve as instruments of punishment. Samba Diallo remembered that one day, in the throes of a mad rage,
the teacher had thrown him to the ground and had
furiously trampled on him, as certain wild beasts do
to their prey.

The teacher was from several points of view a
formidable man. Two occupations filled his life: the
work of the spirit and the work of the field. To the work
of the field he devoted the strict minimum of his time,
and he demanded from the earth no more than he had
to have for his extremely frugal nourishment and that
of his family, not including his pupils. The rest of his
days and nights he consecrated to study, to meditation, to prayer, and to the education and molding of
the young people who had been confided to his care.
He acquitted himself of this task with a passion which
was renowned through all the country of the Diallobé.
Teachers from the most distant regions would come

periodically to visit him and would go away edified. The greatest families of the Diallobé country contended for the honor of sending their sons to him. In general, the teacher would commit himself only after seeing the prospective pupil. When he had refused one, no pressure would ever have made him change his decision. But it might happen that when he had seen a child he would ask that he be allowed to educate him. He had done this in the case of Samba Diallo.

Two years before, the little boy was returning with his father from a long river journey through the Diallobé country. When the boat on which they were traveling drew alongside of the quay, a large group of people assembled in the cabin occupied by Samba Diallo's father. The visitors, filing into the cabin one by one, were coming courteously to salute this son of the countryside whose administrative duties used to keep him far from his own territory for long periods of time.

The teacher was among the last arrivals. When he came into the cabin, Samba Diallo was perched on the knee of his father, who was sitting in an armchair. There were two other men in the room: the director of the regional school, and Samba Diallo's cousin, who was by custom the chief of the province. As the teacher entered the room the three men rose. Samba Diallo's father took the newcomer by the arm and made him sit down in the armchair from which he had just got up.

The three men talked at length on the most diverse topics, but their words would regularly return to a single subject: that of the faith and the greater glory of God.

"Monsieur School Principal," the teacher was saying, "what new good are you teaching men's sons, to make them desert our glowing hearths for the benefit of your schools?"

"Nothing, revered master—or almost nothing," the school principal answered. "The school only teaches men to join wood to wood—to make wooden buildings."

Pronounced in the language of the region, the word "school" means "wood." The three men smiled, with an air of understanding and slight disapproval of this classic play on words in connection with the foreign schools.

"Certainly men ought to learn how to construct dwelling houses that resist the weather," the teacher said.

"Yes," agreed the principal, "that is especially true of those who did not know at all how to build houses before the foreigners came."

"You yourself, chief of the Diallobé, does it not go against the grain with you to send your children to the foreign school?" the teacher asked.

"Unless there is pressure, I shall persist in the refusal to do that, master, if it please God."

"I am quite of your opinion, chief"—it was the principal of the school who was speaking—"I have sent my son to the school only because I could not do otherwise. We have gone there ourselves only under pressure. Our refusal, then, is certain . . . The question is disturbing nevertheless. We reject the foreign school in order to remain ourselves, and to preserve for God the place He holds in our hearts. But have we still enough force to resist the school, and enough substance to remain ourselves?"

The three men fell into a heavy silence. Then Samba Diallo's father, who had remained lost in thought, spoke slowly—as was his habit—fixing his eyes on the floor in front of him, as if he were talking to himself.

"It is certain that nothing pervades our lives with such clamor as the needs of which their school permits the satisfaction. We have nothing left—thanks to them —and it is thus that they hold us. He who wants to live, who wants to remain himself, must compromise. The woodcutters and the metal-workers are triumphant everywhere in the world, and their iron holds us under their law. If it were still only a matter of ourselves, of the conservation of our substance, the problem would have been less complicated: not being able to conquer them, we should have chosen to be wiped out rather than to yield. But we are among the last men on earth to possess God as He veritably is in His Oneness . . . How are we to save Him? When the hand is feeble, the spirit runs great risks, for it is by the hand that the spirit is defended . . ."

"Yes," said the school principal, "but it is also true that the spirit runs great risks when the hand is too strong."

The teacher, wholly given over to his thoughts,

slowly raised his head and considered the three other men.

"Perhaps it is better so? If God has assured their victory over us, it is apparently because we, who are His zealots, have offended Him. For a long time, God's worshippers ruled the world. Did they do it according to His law? I do not know . . . I have learned that in the country of the white man, the revolt against poverty and misery is not distinguished from the revolt against God. They say that the movement is spreading, and that soon, in the world, that same great cry against poverty will drown out the voice of the muezzins. What must have been the misbehavior of those who believe in God if, at the end of their reign over the world, the name of God should arouse the resentment of the starving?"

There was a silence, and then Samba Diallo's father spoke: "Master, what you say is terrible. May God's pity be upon us . . . But must we push our children into their schools?"

"It is certain that their school is the better teacher of how to join wood to wood, and that men should learn how to construct dwelling houses that resist the weather."

"Even at the price of His Sacrifice?"

"I know also that He must be saved. We must build solid dwellings for men, and within those dwellings we must save God. That I know. But do not ask me what should be done tomorrow morning, for that I do not know."

The conversation continued in this way, gloomy

and interrupted by long silences. The Diallobé country, helpless, was turning around and around on itself like a thoroughbred horse caught in a fire.

The teacher's gaze had returned at intervals to Samba Diallo, who sat attentive and silent. Now he pointed to him with his finger and said to his father,

"How old is he?"

"Six years."

"In another year, according to the Law, he must begin his quest for our Lord. I should like to be his guide along that road. Will you allow me? Your son is, I know, of the seed from which the country of the Diallobé produces its masters."

After a pause, he added,

"And the masters of the Diallobé were also the masters whom one-third of the continent chose as guides in the way of God, as well as in human affairs."

The three other men were plunged in meditation. The boy's father spoke:

"If it please God, teacher, I confide my son to you. I shall send him to you at the Glowing Hearth next year, when he will be of the proper age and I shall have prepared him."

So it happened that in the following year Samba Diallo, accompanied by his mother, went back to the teacher, who took possession of him, body and soul. Henceforth, and until he would have completed his classical studies, he belonged no longer to his family.

2

"The peace of God be upon this house. The poor disciple is in quest of his daily pittance."

The sentences, plaintively spoken in a quavering voice by Samba Diallo, were repeated by his three companions. The four youths, shivering in their thin rags of clothing under the blast of the fresh morning wind, stood at the door of the Diallobé chief's spacious dwelling.

"Men of God, reflect upon your approaching death. Awake, Oh, awake! Azrael, Angel of death, is already breaking the earth for you. It is about to rise up at your feet. Men of God, death is not that sly creature it is believed to be, which comes when it is not expected, and conceals itself so well that when it has come there is no longer anyone there."

The three other disciples took up the refrain in chorus:

"Who will feed the poor disciples today? Our fathers are alive, and we beg like orphans. In the name of God, give to those who beg for His Glory. Men who sleep, think of the disciples passing by!"

They fell silent. Samba Diallo spoke alone:

"Men of God, death is not that night which traitorously floods with darkness the innocent and lively ardor of a summer day. It warns, then it mows down in the full mid-day of the intelligence."

Again came the chorus from the other three:

"Men and women who sleep, think of peopling by your benefactions the solitude which will inhabit your tombs. Feed the poor disciples!"

"Men of God, you are warned," Samba Diallo took up the theme again. "One dies lucidly, for death is violence in triumph, negation imposing itself. From now on, may death be familiar to your spirits . . ."

Under the morning wind, Samba Diallo improvised edifying litanies, with interpolations by his comrades, at the closed door of his cousin, the chief of the Diallobé. The disciples would go about so, from door to door, until they had collected victuals enough for their day's nourishment. Tomorrow the same quest would begin again. While seeking God, the disciples would know no other way of supporting life than by begging, whatever their parents' wealth might be.

At last the chief's door opened, and one of his daughters appeared. She bestowed a smile on Samba Diallo, but his countenance remained expressionless. The girl set down on the ground a large plate containing the left-overs from the evening before. The disciples squatted in the dust and set to on their first meal of the day. When they had eaten enough to satisfy their hunger, they put the rest in their wooden bowls, against possible future need. With his bent index finger Samba Diallo thoroughly cleaned the plate, and put the little ball of food, thus recovered, into his mouth. Then he got up and handed the empty plate to his cousin.

"Thank you, Samba Diallo. May you have a good day," she said with a smile.

Samba Diallo did not reply. But Mariam was accustomed to his taciturn and almost tragic humor. When she had turned her back, Demba, the oldest one of the four disciples in Samba Diallo's group, clicked his tongue and burst out laughing, striving after vulgarity.

"If I had a cousin with such dainty dimples," he began.

Then he interrupted himself, for Samba Diallo, who had already taken some steps toward the outer portal, had paused, and was fixing his calm gaze upon the other boy.

"Listen, Samba Diallo," said Demba now. "I know that if it weren't for you my food for the day would be considerably reduced. No one among all the disciples in this countryside would know so well, by inspiring these worthy folk with a salutary fear of Azrael, how to wrest from their selfishness the alms on which we live. This morning, in particular, you have attained a peerless tragic art. I confess that I myself have been on the point of stripping myself of my rags to make you an offering of them."

The other disciples burst out laughing.

"And so?" inquired Samba Diallo, in a voice which he controlled with considerable effort.

"And so, you are the strongest of all the disciples, but you are also the saddest, assuredly. They smile at you after they have fed you, but you remain morose. What is more, you understand nothing of any joke . . ."

"Demba, I have already told you that nothing keeps you here with me," Samba Diallo replied. "You can go away with someone else. I shall not hold it against you."

"What magnanimity, my friends!" Demba spoke mockingly to the other disciples. "What magnanimity! Even when he dismisses me, he dismisses me nobly. 'Go,' he says to me, 'Desert me. And if you die of hunger I shall not hold it against you.'"

The group broke into loud laughter.

"Good, good," declared Demba. "It is understood, great chief. You shall be obeyed."

Samba Diallo gave a start. Demba was seeking a quarrel with him: he could no longer have any doubt of it. All the disciples knew how much it displeased him when anyone called attention to his patrician origin. Certainly he was the best born of all those at the Glowing Hearth, the household of the teacher of the Diallobé. When he begged his food, and, as this morning, went to all homes from the most humble to the most prosperous, everyone, in bringing him the half-spoiled remains of the family meals, would show by a sign or a gesture that under his rags the countryside recognized and was already saluting one of its future leaders. His noble origin weighed upon him: not as a burden he was afraid to carry, but in the manner of a diadem which was too cumbersome and too much in evidence. It was in the manner of an injustice also. He desired nobility, to be sure, but a nobility more discreet, more authentic: not something acquired without effort, but hard-won, and more spiritual than material. He had humiliated and mortified himself, as a means of exercise, and also to show plainly that he insisted on being placed at the same level as all his co-disciples. But nothing had come of this. It seemed, on the contrary, that his comrades bore him a grudge for what, in relation to themselves, they were not far from regarding as the pinnacle of pride. Not a day passed that someone did not remark on the nobility of his bearing or the elegance of his deportment, in spite of the rags in which he was clothed. It even happened that they held a grievance against him for his natural gestures of generosity, and his very frankness. The more he stood guard over himself, the more he was denounced. He was exasperated with it all.

At least his companions in the group had refrained up to the present from making disagreeable remarks. He was silently grateful to them for that, although he had no illusions as to what some of them actually thought. He knew that Demba, notably, was envious of him. This peasant's son, patient and stubborn, harbored the ambition of a sturdy and uncompromising adolescent. "But at least," Samba Diallo was thinking, "Demba has known how to keep quiet up to now. Why should he seek a quarrel with me this morning?"

"Tell me, boys, which one among the other group leaders ought I to follow? Since I am receiving my dismissal from Samba Diallo, I should limit the resultant damage by making a good choice. Let us see . . ."

"Be quiet, Demba; I beg of you, be quiet," Samba Diallo cried.

"Let us see," Demba continued imperturbably. "It is sure, at any rate, that my new leader will not be able to get the best of Samba Diallo in the art of imprecation. For take notice," he went on, always addressing the group, "your prince is not only a prince of the blood. Nothing is lacking to him. He is also a prince of the mind and spirit. What is more, the great teacher himself knows it. You have remarked that? He has a weakness for Samba Diallo."

"You are lying! Be still, Demba—you know very well that you are lying! The teacher cannot have any preference for me, and—"

He broke off and shrugged his shoulders.

He was a few steps away from Demba. The two boys were almost of the same height, but while Samba Diallo—who was now impatiently shifting from one foot to the other—was all long and sinewy lines, Demba was rather inclined to stoutness; he was now standing calm and motionless.

Samba Diallo slowly turned around, walked again to the portal, and went out. In the little street he felt behind him the slow movement of his companions, who were following.

"He has all the qualities, except only one: he is not courageous."

Samba Diallo stopped short, set his wooden bowl on the ground, and went back to Demba.

"I'm not going to fight with you, Dembel," he said.

"No!" the other boy screamed. "Don't call me Dembel. I want no familiarity."

"So be it, Demba. But I do not want to fight. Go or stay, but let us not talk any more about it."

As he spoke, Samba Diallo was standing guard over himself, bent on mastering that vibration which was coursing through his body, and on dissipating that odor of brush fire which was tickling his nostrils.

"Go or stay," he repeated slowly, as if he were speaking in a dream.

Once more he turned his back on Demba and walked away. At this moment his foot struck an obstacle, like a trap set for him. He fell full length on the ground. Someone—he never knew who—had tripped him up.

When he got up, none of those who were there had stirred, but he saw no other person than the one who, before him and still motionless, bore an outline which in a few moments came to represent Demba, but which at present was only the target which his body and all his being had chosen. He was no longer conscious of anything, except that his body, like a butting ram, had catapulted itself upon the target, that the knot of the two entwined bodies had fallen to the ground, and that there was under him something which was struggling and panting, and which he was hitting. His own body, now, was not vibrating any more, but, marvellously supple, was bending and unbending with the blows he was striking, and the mutiny of his body was calmed somewhat with every blow, as every blow restored a little clarity to his benumbed intelligence. Beneath him, the target continued to struggle and pant and was perhaps also striking, but he felt nothing, other than the mastery which his body was progressively imposing upon the target, the peace which the blows he was striking were bringing back to his body, the clarity which they were restoring to his mind. Suddenly the target ceased to move, the clarity was complete. Samba Diallo perceived that silence had fallen, and that two powerful arms had seized him and were forcing him to let his target go.

When he raised his head, his gaze encountered a haughty and imposing visage, muffled in a light veil of white gauze.

They called her the Most Royal Lady. She was sixty years old, and she would have been taken for scarcely forty. Nothing was to be seen of her except her face. The big blue boubou that she wore fell to the ground, and let nothing be seen except the pointed toes of her golden-yellow Turkish slippers, when she walked. The little gauze veil was wound around her throat, covered her head, passed again under her chin, and hung behind. The Most Royal Lady, who could well have been six feet tall, had lost none of her impressive bearing, in spite of her age.

The little white gauze veil clung to the oval of a face of full contours. Samba Diallo had been fascinated by this countenance the first time he had beheld it: it was like a living page from the history of the Diallobé country. Everything that the country treasured of epic tradition could be read there. All the features were in long lines, on the axis of a slightly aquiline nose. The mouth was large and strong, without exaggeration. An extraordinarily luminous gaze bestowed a kind of imperious lustre upon this face. All the rest disappeared under the gauze, which, more than a coiffure would have done, took on here a distinct significance. Islam restrained the formidable turbulence of those features, in the same way that the little veil hemmed them in. Around the eyes and on the cheeks, over all this countenance, there was, as it were, the memory of a youth and a force upon which the rigid blast of an ardent breath was later brutally to blow.

The Most Royal Lady was the older sister of the Diallobé chief. It was said that it was she, more than her brother, whom the countryside feared. If she had ceased her indefatigable excursions on horseback, the memory of her tall silhouette continued no less to hold in obedience the northern tribes who were renowned for their haughty arrogance. The chief of the Diallobé was by nature more inclined to be peaceable. Where he preferred to appeal to understanding, his sister would cut through on the path of authority.

"My brother is not a prince," she was in the habit of saying, "he is a sage." Or, again, "The sovereign should never argue in the public light of day, and the people should not see his face in the night's darkness."

She had pacified the North by her firmness. The tribes subjugated by her extraordinary personality had been kept in obedience by her prestige. It was the North that had given her the name "the Most Royal Lady."

Now there was complete silence among the disciples, turned to stone as if by the Gorgon's head.

"I have warned your great fool of a father that your place is not at the teacher's hearth," she said. "When you are not fighting like a yokel you are terrorizing all the region by your imprecations against life. The teacher is trying to kill the life in you. But I am going to put an end to all that. Go wait for me at the house . . ."

Having spoken, she went on her way.

When the teacher saw Samba Diallo come in that evening, covered with red spots and wearing new clothes, he fell into a terrible rage.

"Come here," he summoned, when he saw the boy still at a distance. "Approach, son of a prince. I swear I will reduce the arrogance of the Diallobé in you!"

He took off his clothes as far as his belt and beat him slowly and furiously. Samba Diallo submitted, inert to the storm. Then the teacher called the poorest and most badly dressed of the boys at the Glowing Hearth, and ordered him to change his worn clothing for Samba Diallo's new garments—which was done to the disciple's great joy. Samba Diallo put on his comrade's rags with indifference.

All the disciples had come back. Each of them had taken his writing-tablet again and, in his proper place, had rejoined the large circle. The Word, intoned by all the immature voices, rose, sonorous and beneficent to the heart of the teacher, as he sat in the centre of the group. He considered Samba Diallo.

The boy gave him complete satisfaction, save on

one point. The old man's piercing scrutiny had disclosed in this youth what seemed to him—unless combatted early—the misfortune of the Diallobé nobility, and through them of the Diallobé country as a whole. The teacher believed profoundly that the adoration of God was not compatible with any exaltation of man. But, at the bottom of all nobility there is a basis of paganism. Nobility is the exaltation of man, faith is before all else humility, if not humiliation. The teacher thought that man had no reason to exalt himself, save definitely in the adoration of God. Now it was true—though he fought against the feeling—that he loved Samba Diallo as he had never loved any disciple. His harshness toward the boy was in ratio to his impatience to rid him of all his moral weaknesses, and to make him the masterpiece of his own long career. He had educated and developed numerous generations of adolescents, and he knew that he was now near death. But, at the same time as himself, he felt that the country of the Diallobé was dying from the assault of strangers come from beyond the sea. Before departing this life, the teacher would try to leave to the Diallobé such a man as the country's great past had produced.

The teacher recalled former years. In the time of his adolescence the children of the great families—of whom he was one—would still be living their time of youth far from the aristocratic milieu from which they had sprung, anonymous and poor among the people, and on this people's alms.

At the end of this period of companionship, they would return from their long peregrination among books and men, both learned and democratic, seasoned in body and clear of mind.

The teacher lingered in meditation, reawakened to the memory of the vanished days when the country drew its sustenance from God and from the strong liquor of its traditions.

That evening, as he was silently praying at the door of his little cabin, the teacher suddenly felt a presence near him. When he raised his eyes his gaze encountered "a noble and haughty countenance," as men described her, "a woman's head enveloped in a light little veil of white gauze."

"Does peace reign in your dwelling, teacher of the Diallobé?" the woman asked.

"I give thanks to God, Most Royal Lady. Does peace reign in your house also?"

"May thanks be rendered to the Lord."

She removed her shoes three steps away from the teacher and took the place on the rug which he pointed out to her.

"Master, I have come to see you in the matter of Samba Diallo. This morning I heard the litanies he was improvising."

"I too heard them. They are beautiful and profound."

"I was frightened by them. I know very well that the thought of death keeps the believer on guard, and I count the anxiety which it sets in our hearts as among Our Lord's benefactions. I know also what pride

I ought to feel in the gifts of intelligence which it has pleased Our Lord to impart to my young cousin."

"Yes." The teacher spoke slowly, as if he were talking to himself. "He is not one of the stupid believers wakened by his morning sermons, in the heart of whom there is a feeling of admiration mingled with the great terror he arouses."

"Nevertheless, master, I am disturbed. This child speaks of death in terms which do not belong to his years. I come to ask you humbly, for the love of this disciple whom you cherish, to remember, in your work of edification, his age."

Having said this, the Most Royal Lady fell silent. The teacher also remained silent for a long time. When he spoke, it was to ask a question:

"Most Royal Lady, do you remember your father?"

"Yes, master," she responded simply—surprised nevertheless.

"Less well than I, for I knew him long before you, and I always approached him closely. But do you remember the state of mind in which he died?"

"Certainly I remember."

"Less well than I, again, for it was I who spoke the prayer for the dying over him, and I who buried him. Permit me to call him to mind this evening—and this is not irrelevant to what we are talking about."

Again, the teacher was silent for a moment. Then he went on:

"He suffered for a long time alone, without anyone's knowing of it, for he had made no change in his way of life. One day he had me summoned. When I arrived, after he had given me a long greeting and we had talked as we were accustomed to do, he got up, went to a chest which he opened, and took out a large piece of cambric. 'This is my shroud,' he said to me, 'and I should like you to tell me the ritual fashion in which it should be cut.' I was seeking to probe his gaze. The peace and the gravity which I observed there reduced to nothing, in my mind, all the vain words of protest which I had been about to pronounce. I congratulate myself for having done away with them, so much so, even today, that I feel the absurdity of such words in the presence of this man who dominated death with all his great stature. I obeyed him, then, and gave him the directions from the Book. He cut his shroud with his own hands. When he had finished, he asked me to accompany him to a retired spot in his house, and there asked me to indicate in his presence to his slave Mbara the motions and the details of the funeral dressing. We came back into his room, then, and talked together for a long time, as if pain were not visibly tormenting his body. When I got up to leave, he asked me to be kind enough to be present when the hour arrived.

"Two days later they came from him to seek me. I found a silent and dismayed family, a house full of people. Your father was in his bedroom, lying on a mat on the floor, surrounded by a number of persons. It was the only time when he did not rise as I entered. He smiled at me, and after greeting me he asked me to bring together all those whom he had called to his house. 'I beg them to tell me before I die,' he said, 'what I could

have owed to them and what I might have forgotten to
render in payment. If there is one who holds the memory of an injustice from me, may I be told of it and may
I make public apology. Of all, I ask that I may be par-
doned for the private misdeeds which I may have com-
mitted and for the great misdeed stemming from my
office as chief of the Diallobé. Hurry, if you please. I
await you.'

" 'Have they forgiven me?' he asked, as I returned,
and everyone saw the anxiety that tore him at this time.
I replied that all had been forgiven. He put that question to me three times. After that he had the strength to
greet all those who were around him. He begged that
my arm might be strong, wishing that I would ask the
same of his; and he died pronouncing the name of God.
Most Royal Lady, that was a chief, your father, who
showed to me—to me the interpreter of the Book—how
a man should die. I should like to transmit this boon to
his little nephew."

"I revere my father, and the memory you have of
him," the Most Royal Lady responded, "but I believe
that the time has come to teach our sons to live. I fore-
see that they will have to do with a world of the living,
in which the values of death will be scoffed at and
bankrupt."

"No, Madame. Those are the ultimate values,
which will still have their place at the pillow of the last
human being. You see that I am injuring the life in your
young cousin, and you take a stand against me. For me,
however, the task is not agreeable, or easy. I beg you
not to tempt me, and to leave its firmness to my hand.

After this deep wounding, from a hand that is fatherly,
I promise you that this child will never wound himself.
You will see from what stature he too will dominate life,
and death."

3

Only the teacher had remained in the silent cabin. With twilight, the disciples had taken flight in quest of their evening meal. Nothing stirred except, above the teacher, the swallows fluttering among the smoke-blackened lattices of the thatched roof. Slowly, the teacher rose. The crackling of all his joints, stiff from rheumatism, made a sound which was mingled with the sigh wrested from him by the effort to get up. In spite of the solemnity of the hour—the teacher was rising in order to pray—the teacher could not restrain an inner laughter over this grotesque misery of his body, which was now balking at prayer. "You will get up, and you will pray," he said to himself. "Your groanings and your noises will avail you nothing." This scene had become classic. The teacher was failing physically. More every day, his body emphasized this sorry propensity to remain glued to the earth. For example, he no longer had confidence in the joints of his feet, which refused him all obedience.

He had resolved to do without them, and his knee joints had become dry and stiff like the dead wood that the disciples burned. For this reason, the teacher's gait had taken on the curious rolling motion of web-footed birds. Every time he bent over or straightened up he had to pull himself together again, so as not to take account of the pressing pain that he felt at the level of his kidneys. The joints of his knees and his elbows were still functioning, though they crackled in an incongruous fashion. Paradoxically, all this suffering, and this rebellion of his body, aroused in the teacher's mood a gayety which left him perplexed. Although he was bent in two with pain, he had trouble in remaining serious, as if the grotesque figure he was watching were not his own. Once more, this laughter in him was held back. At this moment the teacher, who had raised his two arms toward the east, to begin his prayer, interrupted himself, suddenly sobered by a suspicion: was this laughter not impious? "Perhaps," he reflected, "it is an evil vanity which inflates me so." He meditated for a moment. "No," he thought, "my laughter is loving. I laugh because my old companion does pranks with the cracking of his joints. But his will is better than ever. I believe that even when he is completely bound to the earth, all the length of his body, his will must still be very good. He will pray, I love him very much; let us continue." Restored to serenity, he recovered himself and began his prayer.

When the emissary came, the teacher did not see him. He merely heard a voice at his back:

"Great master, the chief hopes that you will do him the honor of a visit, if your high preoccupations leave you the leisure . . ."

Slowly and as if regretfully, the teacher's thought detached itself from the lofty summits it had been contemplating. In truth, the teacher was returning from far away.

"So long as my body obeys me I shall always respond to the chief," he said. "So tell him that I am following you, if it please God."

When he entered the chief's room he found him still in prayer. He sat down on the mat, took out his beads, and waited.

Spiral curves of odorous incense were escaping from the big white bed and were slightly dimming the light from the storm lamp. Everything in this room was clean and pure. The chief, clothed in a great white boubou, was now seated motionless, facing the east; without doubt it was the day's final witness. The teacher settled himself in his place and, in thought, repeated with the chief, perhaps for the millionth time, the great profession of faith:

"I bear witness that there is no god but God, and I bear witness that Mohammed is His prophet . . ."

The chief finished his prayer. He turned toward the teacher and with both hands extended saluted him at length.

"I should have given myself a pleasure and performed a duty in coming to visit you, if you had not one day expressly forbidden it," the chief said. "You told me, as I remember, 'Stability is at the same time a privilege and a duty for you princes of this world.'"

"In effect," the teacher rejoined, "you are the landmark and you are the recourse. Put that a little to the test, chief of the Diallobé. Has one man alone the right to monopolize what belongs to all? I answer, No. If the landmark moves, where do men go?"

"They do not know."

"It is the same with the recourse, the presence of which reassures them."

The two men, the similarity of whose natures brought them together on essential points, were trying out once more the solid ground of their mutual admiration.

"Master," the chief asked, "am I a landmark sufficiently fixed, a recourse sufficiently stable?"

"You are."

"Just so. I am the authority. Where I establish myself, the earth yields and is furrowed under my weight. I dig myself in, and men come to me. Master, they believe me to be a mountain."

"You are that."

"I am a poor thing, who trembles, and who does not know . . ."

"It is true, you are that also."

"More and more, men come to me. What should I say to them?"

The teacher knew what the chief was going to talk to him about. He had approached the subject with him a thousand times. The men of the Diallobé wanted to learn "how better to join wood to wood." The mass of the country had made the reverse choice to that of the teacher. While the latter was setting at naught the stiffness of his joints, the pressure on his loins, setting his cabin at naught, and recognizing the reality only of Him toward Whom his thought mounted with delight at every instant, the people of the Diallobé were each day a little more anxious about the stability of their dwellings, the unhealthy state of their bodies. The Diallobé wanted more substance . . .

Substance, weight . . . When his thought abutted on these words, the teacher shuddered. Weight! Everywhere he encountered weight. When he wanted to pray, weight opposed him, the heavy load of his daily cares over the upward sweep of his thought toward God, the inert and more and more sclerotic mass of his body over his will to rise, then to abase himself, then to rise again, in the motions of prayer. There were also other aspects of weight which, even as the Evil One, revealed diverse visages: the distraction of the disciples, the brilliant enchantments of their young imagination, as much as those essential properties of weight that were desperately eager to hold them to the earth, to keep them far from truth.

He answered the chief's question:

"Tell them that they are gourds."

The teacher repressed a smile as he spoke. In general, the mischievousness of his thought amused him. The chief, however, was listening attentively, knowing by long custom what bases he must find for the venerable man's changes of mood.

"The gourd is of a droll nature," the teacher went on after a long pause. "When young, it has no other vocation than to achieve weight, no other desire than to attach itself lovingly to the earth. It finds the perfect realization of itself in weight. Then one day everything changes. The gourd wants to take flight. It reabsorbs itself, hollows itself out, as much as it can. Its happiness is a function of its vacuity, of the sonority of its response when a breath stirs it. The gourd is right in both instances."

"Master, where are the gourds of the Diallobé?"

"That is for the gardener to answer, not for me."

The chief remained silent for a moment.

"If I told them to go to the new school," he said at last, "they would go *en masse*. They would learn all the ways of joining wood to wood which we do not know. But, learning, they would also forget. Would what they would learn be worth as much as what they would forget? I should like to ask you: can one learn *this* without forgetting *that*, and is what one learns worth what one forgets?"

"At the Glowing Hearth, what we teach the children is God. What they forget is themselves, their bodies, and the futile dream which hardens with age and stifles the spirit. So what they learn is worth infinitely more than what they forget."

"If I do not tell the Diallobé to go to the new school, they will not go. Their houses will fall into ruins, their children will die or be reduced to slavery. Extreme poverty will be entrenched among them, and their hearts will be filled with resentment."

"Extreme poverty is, down here, the principal enemy of God."

"Nevertheless, master, if I understand you aright, poverty is also the absence of weight, of substance. How are the Diallobé to be given knowledge of the arts and the use of arms, the possession of riches and the health of the body, without at the same time weighing them down, dulling their minds?"

"Give them the weight, my brother. Otherwise, I declare that soon there will remain neither person nor thing in the country. There are more deaths than births among the Diallobé. You yourself, master, your hearths are becoming extinct."

It was the Most Royal Lady speaking. She had come into the room without making a sound, as was her custom. She had left her Turkish slippers behind the door. This was the hour of her daily visit to her brother. Now she took her place on the mat, facing the two men.

"I am delighted to find you here, master," she said. "Perhaps we are going to bring matters into focus this evening."

"I do not see how, Madame. We move along parallel lines, and both are inflexible."

"Yes, indeed, master. My brother is the living heart of this country, but you are its conscience. Envelop yourself in shadow, retire into your own heart, and nothing, I declare to you, will bring good fortune to the Diallobé. Your house is the most scantily furnished in the countryside, your body the most emaciated, your appearance the most fragile. But no one has a sovereign authority over this country which equals yours."

The teacher felt terror overcoming him, gently, in time with this woman's speech. He had never dared to admit very plainly what she was saying, but he knew it to be the truth.

Man always wishes for prophets to absolve him from his insufficiencies, but why should they have chosen him, a creature who did not even know what to abide by on his own account? At this moment his thought went back to his inner laughter at the solemn instant of his prayer. "I do not even know why I laughed," he reflected. "Was it because in conquering the weakness of my body I was conscious of giving pleasure to my Lord, or was it from vanity, and nothing else? I do not know how to settle this question. I do not know myself . . . I do not know myself, and it is I to whom they choose to look. For they do look to me. All these unhappy people spy on me, and, like chameleons, take on for themselves the color of my moods. But I do not want that: I do not want it! I shall compromise myself. I shall commit some notably unworthy action, if it please God, to show them who I am. Yes . . ."

"My brother, is it not true," the Most Royal Lady was saying, "that without the light of those hearths nothing could be done for the happiness and welfare of the Diallobé people? And you know very well, great master, that there is no means of escape that could liberate you."

"Madame, God has closed the sublime line of His envoys with our prophet Mohammed, may blessing be upon him. The last messenger has transmitted to us that ultimate Word in which everything has been said. Only the insensate expect anything further."

"And along with them the famished, the sick, the enslaved. My brother, tell the master that the country is awaiting his acquiescence."

"Before you came in," the chief responded to his sister, "the master had just heard me say, 'I am a poor thing, that trembles and does not know.' This slow vertigo in which we turn about on ourselves, my country and I—will it come to an end? Most Royal Lady, tell me that your choice will be of greater worth than the vertigo: that it will cure us of it and not, on the contrary, hasten our ruin. You are strong. The whole country lies under your great shadow. Give me your faith."

"I have none. I merely draw conclusions from premises which I have not desired. A hundred years ago our grandfather, along with all the inhabitants of this countryside, was awakened one morning by an uproar arising from the river. He took his gun and, followed by all the élite of the region, he flung himself upon the newcomers. His heart was intrepid, and to him the value of liberty was greater than the value of life. Our grandfather, and the élite of the country with him, was defeated. Why? How? Only the newcomers know. We must ask them: we must go to learn from them the art of conquering without being in the right. Furthermore, the conflict has not yet ceased. The foreign school is the new form of the war which those who have come here are waging, and we must send our élite there, expecting that all the country will follow them. It is well that once more the élite should lead the way. If there is a risk, they are the best prepared to cope successfully with it, because they are the most firmly attached to what they are. If there is good to be drawn from it, they should also be the first to acquire that. This is what I wish you to say, my brother. And, since the master is present, I should like to add another word: our determination to send the noble youth to the foreign school will never be followed by the people unless we begin by sending our own children there. So I think that your children, my brother, as well as our cousin Samba Diallo, should start the procession."

As he heard these words the teacher's heart was strangely convulsed.

"Lord, can it be that I am so much attached to this child?" he prayed in his thought. "Then at my hearth I have preferences . . . It is so, Oh, my God! Forgive me . . . And they look to me, wishing me to be their guide."

"Samba Diallo is your child," he said to the chief. "I shall give him back to you as soon as you express that wish."

The teacher's voice was a little husky as he gave voice to this decision.

"In any case, that is another problem," responded the chief.

4

Samba Diallo had a vague prescience of the importance of the problem of which he was the centre. He
had often seen the Most Royal Lady stand up, alone,
against the men of the Dialloubé family. At the moment
she was always victorious, because no one dared hold
out against her for long. She was the first-born. So then
the Most Royal Lady carried off Samba Diallo, almost
by force, and kept him in her home, sending back all the
emissaries that the chief despatched to her. She kept
Samba Diallo for a solid week, making much of him in
every way, as if to correct the effects of the education
of the Glowing Hearth, by going to whatever extremes
she could.

Samba Diallo let himself be pampered with apparently the same profound equanimity of soul as when he
submitted to the hearth's bad treatment. Incontestably,
he felt happy in the Most Royal Lady's house. But
nevertheless he did not experience that plenitude of
spirit he had felt at the hearth, which would set his
heart to beating, for instance, when under the teacher's
formidable eye he would pronounce the Word. Life at
the teacher's hearth was unceasingly painful, and held
a suffering which was not of the body alone.

It was acquired like an aftermath of authenticity.
When at the end of a week the Most Royal Lady

let him go, satiated with over-indulgence, the chief of
the Diallobé and the teacher subjected him to re-
doubled severity, as if to make him expiate that week
of well-being.

It was in the course of one of those weeks of concentrated severity that he found a retreat where no one
would ever have dreamed of coming to look for him.

For some days, now, it had been extremely painful
for him to live in the village. The teacher had become
eccentric in his behavior, and it seemed to Samba Diallo
that he was at once less severe and more distant. It was
only the Most Royal Lady who did not seem to avoid
him a little. This situation persisted for such a long time,
as the boy saw it, that one evening when he could not
stand it any longer he made his way to his refuge.

"Old Rella," he was thinking, as he stretched himself out by her side. And then, "Good evening, Old
Rella, if you hear me."

It was thus that he announced himself every time.
He scarcely doubted that she heard him.

Naturally, she had never made any answer, and
this was a weighty argument in favor of doubt. Samba
Diallo even knew that within these low heaps of earth
rested only little piles of bones. One day when he was
drawing near to Old Rella he had inadvertently stepped
on a mound similar to that beneath which his silent
friend reposed, and it had yielded under him. When he
raised his foot he noticed an excavation at the bottom
of the hollow he had just formed there. He leaned over,
and in the dim light he perceived a whiteness that was
gleaming slightly. So he had learned that under all

these mounds there was no longer any flesh, no more open eyes, ears attentive to the step of passers-by, as he had imagined, but only laid-out chains, as it were, of whitened bones. His heart had beaten a little faster: he was thinking of Old Rella. So even the eyes, even the flesh, would disappear? Perhaps in sufficiently ancient abiding-places the bones themselves would vanish? Samba Diallo never verified this last, but he remained convinced of it. When the boy became aware that Old Rella had been physically engulfed, so to speak, it had the effect of bringing her closer to him. What he lost in her material presence it seemed to him that he gained in another way, and this was richer.

He began to address her, silently:

"Old Rella, good evening. If you hear me, Old Rella . . . But if you do not hear me, what are you doing? Where can you be? This very morning I saw your daughter Coumba. You loved Coumba very much. Why have you never come back to see her? Yet you loved her very much. Or perhaps they are holding you somewhere. Tell me, Old Rella, are they holding you somewhere? Is it Azrael, perhaps? No, Azrael could do nothing. He is only a messenger. Or perhaps, Old Rella, you do not love Coumba any more? Perhaps you are no longer able to love . . ."

Samba Diallo felt no fear of Old Rella. Rather, she caused him a certain mental disquiet, and tormented his curiosity. He knew that she was no longer flesh, nor bone, nor anything that was material. What had she become? Old Rella could not have ceased, finally, to be. Old Rella . . . She had left traces. When one has

left fat Coumba behind, and when one used to love fat
Coumba as Old Rella had loved her, one cannot have
ceased to be. How can the memory of this love still en-
dure if the love itself has completely, finally, ceased?
For the memory still lived in Coumba. From time to
time she wept. Samba Diallo had seen her weeping
one evening as she came home from the cemetery. Why
should she weep if everything was finished, finally?
Everything was not finished . . . But why, then, had
Old Rella never come back? He, Samba Diallo, knew
that he loved his father and mother so much that if he
should ever die before them, and it might be possible
for him to return, or make them a sign in some fashion,
he would manifest himself to tell them what he had
seen, to give them news of Paradise. Unless? . . . Yes,
perhaps, perhaps one does forget. But now Samba Diallo
felt himself on the verge of tears, merely in thinking
that he might be able to forget his father, and his
mother too, both of whom he loved so much. "Old Rella,
Old Rella, does one forget?"

He banished this idea, and thought of Paradise.
Yes, that was the explanation: Paradise. Whatever
might be the reason for their silence, their absence, it
could only be beneficent, it could only belong to Paradise. They had not disappeared into an obscure nothingness, they neither felt hatred nor were they forgetful.
They simply were in Paradise.

For a long time, near his dead friend, the child reflected on the eternal mystery of death, and, on his own
count, rebuilt Paradise in a thousand ways. When sleep
came to him he had grown entirely serene again, for he

had found the answer: Paradise was built with the Words that he used to recite, the same glowing lights, the same deep and mysterious shadows, the same enchantment, the same power.

How long did he sleep thus, close to that absolute which fascinated him and which he did not know?

He was awakened with a start by a loud cry, which set him to trembling violently. When he opened his eyes he was already surrounded by people. A storm lantern held at arm's length lighted the mausoleum over the mound where Old Rella lay. The entrance to it was blocked by an increasing company of men. Samba Diallo closed his eyes again. He heard words.

"But it is Samba Diallo . . . What can he be doing here?"

"Perhaps he is ill? A child in the cemeteries, at night . . ."

"We must call the chief."

Samba Diallo had quietly covered his face again with a fold of the ragged clothing he wore. Silence fell around him. He felt that someone had leaned over him and uncovered his face. He opened his eyes, and his gaze encountered that of the chief of the Diallobé.

"See, my child, don't be afraid. What is it? What are you doing here?"

"I am not afraid any more. A great cry woke me. I must have frightened someone."

"Get up. How long have you been here?"

"For a long time . . . I do not know."

"You are not afraid?"

"No."

"That is good. Get up. I am going to take you back to the house, where you will stay from now on."

"I want to go to the Glowing Hearth."

"Very well. I will take you back to the Glowing Hearth."

The men around, who had come to a night interment, slowly dispersed. They were mildly amused by the misadventure which had befallen Hamadi, Coumba's husband. It was he who, discovering the form of Samba Diallo stretched out against the tomb of Hamadi's mother-in-law, had cried out. Why had he done so?

There was a brief muttering, then a muttering that was long drawn out. The tone changed, it rose in the scale, there was a brief muttering, then a long muttering. The two tones blended, there were two simultaneous voices, one long, the other short.

Sudden movements began to be noted in the surge of sound. Something unguessed started to rush through each muttering's whole spinning sound. The spinnings were multiplied. The drive was a paroxysm. Samba Diallo woke up. The earth was being shaken by beatings on the tom-tom.

Samba Diallo remembered. "This is the day," he said to himself, "that the Most Royal Lady has convoked the Diallobé. The tom-tom is calling them."

He got up from the beaten earthen soil where he had been sleeping, made a brief toilette, prayed, and went out of the teacher's house to go to the village square where the Diallobé were assembling. The square was already full of people. When he reached it, Samba Diallo was surprised to see that there were as many women there as men. It was the first time he had seen anything like that. The gathering formed a large rectangle, several rows thick, the women on two sides, the men on the other two. They were all talking in low tones, and this made a permeating murmur, like the voice of the wind. Suddenly the murmur fell away. One side of the rectangle opened, and the Most Royal Lady entered the arena.

It was in the midst of a great silence, now, that she spoke:

"People of the Diallobé, I salute you."

A diffuse and powerful hum of sound answered her. She went on:

"I have done something which is not pleasing to us and which is not in accordance with our customs. I have asked the women to come to this meeting today. We Diallobé hate that, and rightly, for we think that the women should remain at home. But more and more we shall have to do things which we hate doing, and which do not accord with our customs. It is to exhort you to do one of those things that I have asked you to come to this meeting today.

"I come here to say this to you: I, the Most Royal Lady, do not like the foreign school. I detest it. My opinion, nevertheless, is that we should send our children there."

There was a muttering among the crowd. The Most Royal Lady waited until it had died down, then she continued calmly:

"I must tell you this: neither my brother, your chief, nor the teacher of the Diallobé has yet taken a stand in this matter. They are seeking the truth. They are right. As for me, I am like your baby, Coumba." She pointed to the child, while they all watched her. "Look at him. He is learning to walk. He does not know where he is going. He only knows that he should lift one foot and put it ahead, then that he should lift the other and put it in front of the first."

Always with her eyes on her audience, the Most Royal Lady turned in another direction:

"Ardo Diallobé, you said to me yesterday, 'Speech may be suspended, but life is not suspended.' That is very true. Look at Coumba's baby."

All those present remained motionless, as if petrified. Only the Most Royal Lady stirred. In the centre of the company she was like a seed in its pod.

"The school in which I would place our children will kill in them what today we love and rightly conserve with care. Perhaps the very memory of us will die in them. When they return from the school, there may be those who will not recognize us. What I am proposing is that we should agree to die in our children's hearts and that the foreigners who have defeated us should fill the place, wholly, which we shall have left free."

She was silent again, though no murmur had interrupted her. Samba Diallo heard the sound of someone sniffling near him, and raising his head he perceived two great tears coursing down the rough cheeks of the master of the blacksmiths.

"But, people of the Diallobé," she continued after a

pause, "remember our fields when the rainy season is approaching. We love our fields very much, but what do we do then? We plough them up and burn them: we kill them. In the same way, recall this: what do we do with our reserves of seed when the rain has fallen? We would like to eat them, but we bury them in the earth.

"Folk of the Diallobé, with the arrival of the foreigners has come the tornado which announces the great hibernation of our people. My opinion—I, the Most Royal Lady—is that our best seeds and our dearest fields—those are our children. Does anyone wish to speak?"

No one answered.

"Then peace be upon you, people of the Diallobé," the Most Royal Lady concluded.

5

The country of the Diallobé was not the only one which had been awakened by a great clamor early one day. The entire black continent had had its moment of clamor.

Strange dawn! The morning of the Occident in black Africa was spangled over with smiles, with cannon shots, with shining glass beads. Those who had no history were encountering those who carried the world on their shoulders. It was a morning of accouchement: the known world was enriching itself by a birth that took place in mire and blood.

From shock, the one side made no resistance. They were a people without a past, therefore without memory. The men who were landing on their shores were white, and mad. Nothing like them had ever been known. The deed was accomplished before the people were even conscious of what had happened.

Some among the Africans, such as the Diallobé, brandished their shields, pointed their lances, and aimed their guns. They were allowed to come close, then the cannon were fired. The vanquished did not understand . . .

Others wanted to parley. They were given a choice: friendship or war. Very sensibly, they chose friendship. They had no experience at all.

The result was the same, nevertheless, everywhere.

Those who had shown fight and those who had surrendered, those who had come to terms and those who had been obstinate—they all found themselves, when the day came, checked by census, divided up, classified, labeled, conscripted, administrated.

For the newcomers did not know only how to fight. They were strange people. If they knew how to kill with effectiveness, they also knew how to cure, with the same art. Where they had brought disorder, they established a new order. They destroyed and they constructed. On the black continent it began to be understood that their true power lay not in the cannons of the first morning, but rather in what followed the cannons.

Thus, behind the gunboats, the clear gaze of the Most Royal Lady of the Diallobé had seen the new school.

The new school shares at the same time the characteristics of cannon and of magnet. From the cannon it draws its efficacy as an arm of combat. Better than the cannon, it makes conquest permanent. The cannon compels the body, the school bewitches the soul. Where the cannon has made a pit of ashes and of death, in the sticky mold of which men would not have rebounded from the ruins, the new school establishes peace. The morning of rebirth will be a morning of benediction through the appeasing virtue of the new school.

From the magnet, the school takes its radiating force. It is bound up with a new order, as a magnetic stone is bound up with a field. The upheaval of the life of man within this new order is similar to the overturn of certain physical laws in a magnetic field. Men are seen to be composing themselves, conquered, along the lines of invisible and imperious forces. Disorder is organized, rebellion is appeased, the mornings of resentment resound with songs of a universal thanksgiving.

Only such an upheaval in the natural order can explain how, without either of them wanting it, the new man and the new school come together just the same. For neither of them wants the other. The man does not want the school because in order that he may live— that is, be free, feed and clothe himself—it imposes upon him the necessity of sitting henceforth, for the required period, upon its benches. No more does the school want the man because in order to survive—that is, extend itself and take roots where its necessity has landed it—it is obliged to take account of him.

When the Lacroix family arrived in the little Negro town of L., they found a school there. It was on the classroom benches of this school filled with little black children that Jean Lacroix made the acquaintance of Samba Diallo.

On the morning of their fifteenth day at L., M. Lacroix had taken his two children, Jean and Georgette, to the school of the little town. At Pau, the little boy and girl had not gone above the lower grades. Here, the class of M. N'Diaye corresponded broadly to what they needed.

The story of Samba Diallo is a serious story. If it had been a gay recital, we should have told you of the bewilderment of the two white children, on the first

morning of their sojourn among little Negroes, in finding themselves in the presence of so many black faces.
Such were the peripheries of this vast movement of approach that Jean and his sister felt it was closing in
about them, little by little, like some fantastic and patient ballet. What was their childish surprise, one might
have said, to realize after some time, how much, under
their kinky heads and their dark skins, their new school-
mates resembled those they had left behind in Pau . . .

But nothing more will be said of all that, because
these memories would revive others, all of them also
happy, and would bring gayety to this recital of which
the profound truth is wholly sad.

Long afterward, thinking of this, Jean Lacroix believed that he remembered perceiving this sadness—
though in a diffuse and imprecise way—from his first
moments of contact with Samba Diallo.

It was in M. N'Diaye's class that he first felt this. In
this class he had had, as it were, the impression of a
point where all noises were absorbed, where all rustling
sounds were lost. One might have said that somewhere in the ambient air there was a break in continu-
ity. So, when it happened that the whole class would be
laughing or shrieking, his attentive ear would perceive
something like a pit of silence not far from where he sat.
As the hour of dismissal approached, and a quiver
would run through all the benches, slates would be
shaken and then surreptitiously put away, and there
would be a dropping of things that had been gathered
together, Jean's whole person would feel at the heart of
this agitation something like a break of peace.

As a matter of fact, although he might have noticed it from the outset, it was only after some ten days in M. N'Diaye's classroom that Jean became clearly conscious of this universal false note. From that moment, all his senses were on the alert.

One morning M. N'Diaye was questioning the class and had—fairly enough—taken the presence of Jean and Georgette as pretext for an interrogation on the geography and history of France. The interchange between master and pupils was sustained and swift. Then suddenly a silence, an embarrassed silence, fell upon the class.

"Let us see, my children," M. N'Diaye insisted, "Pau is in a department of which it is the capital. What is this department? You remember Pau?"

Jean, to whom the question was not addressed, perceived very clearly, then, that someone not far from him was not embarrassed by this silence, someone was enjoying this silence and prolonging it at his pleasure, someone who could break it, who was about to break it. He slowly turned his head and, for the first time, observed his neighbor on the right, the pupil who with Georgette and himself shared the first table of the central row. It was like a revelation. The pit of silence, the break of peace—it was this boy! He who at this moment was attracting all glances by a sort of restrained radiation, he whom Jean had not noticed but whose presence in this class had troubled him from the first days . . .

Jean observed him in profile. He could do so at ease, for the other had raised his head and was fixing all his attention on M. N'Diaye. The class was looking

at him, and he was looking at the teacher. He seemed
tense. His countenance, the regularity of which Jean
noted, was beaming. Jean had the impression that if he
leaned over and looked straight at his companion,
he could read on his face—so great was its effulgence—
the answer that M. N'Diaye was expecting. But, one
might say in spite of this tension and this radiation,
nothing about the boy stirred. Jean was later to think
back and realize that he never raised his hand, though
when a pupil wished to answer a question, it was the
custom for him to raise his hand and snap his fingers.
Jean's neighbor remained motionless and tense, as if he
had his heart in his mouth. M. N'Diaye turned toward
him, and Jean noted something like a muscular relaxa-
tion on the other's part. He smiled, and had the air of
being confused. Then he got up.

"The department of which Pau is the capital is the
Basses-Pyrénées. Pau is the city in which Henri IV was
born."

His voice was clear-cut and his language correct.
He was speaking to M. N'Diaye, but Jean had the impression that he was speaking to the class, that it was to
them that he was giving account.

When he had finished speaking he sat down again,
on a sign from M. N'Diaye. Jean was still staring at
him. He noticed that this embarrassed the other boy,
and gave himself over to the contemplation of his slate.

Having paused for a moment, the class went back
to its routine. Then only did Jean remember that it was
not by chance that he was sitting near Samba Diallo.
He recalled that when he arrived he had wished to lead

his sister to a table where there were two vacant places, as he had noticed. M. N'Diaye had intervened, and had had them sit at the first table, next to Samba Diallo.

When the noon bell had rung, when M. N'Diaye had dismissed his pupils and Georgette and Jean had gone out, it was impossible for the latter to find Samba Diallo again. Jean was standing on his tiptoes, looking about him on all sides, when someone touched his shoulder. He turned around. It was Ammar Lô, the first boy in the class that he had made friends with.

"Who are you looking for, the Diallobé?"

"Who is that?"

"But that is your neighbor, Samba Diallo."

Jean was surprised and a little put out that Ammar Lô should have guessed his thought. He did not reply.

"Don't wait any longer for Samba Diallo. He has gone," Ammar Lô volunteered. Then he turned his back and went away.

M. Lacroix had come in a car to get his children. When Jean went back to school in the afternoon Samba Diallo was not there, and he was conscious of some chagrin.

The next day was Thursday.* Jean did not go out in the morning, but in the afternoon he betook himself to his father's office in the Résidence du Cercle. He knocked at the door and went in. There were two people in the room he entered, occupying two separate desks. One of them was his father. He made his way toward him, but he was looking at the other man, who was a Negro.

* Thursday is the holiday in French schools. Tr.

He was a tall man, something which one noticed at once, even though he was seated. The boubous he wore were white, and full-cut. Under his clothing one sensed a stature which was powerful without being fleshy. His hands were at once large and finely molded. His bearing helped to give a hieratic posture to his head, which one would have said was cut out of gleaming black sandstone. Why, on looking at him, did Jean think of a certain engraving in his history textbook, which showed a knight of the Middle Ages clad in his dalmatic vestments? The man, on whose face there was a lightly sketched smile, slowly turned his head so that his glance followed the boy. Jean, for his part, was watching him so attentively that he almost bumped into a chair.

"Well, Jean, say good afternoon to this gentleman," his father said.

Jean took a few steps toward the man, who smiled once more and held out his hand—a gesture which spread his wide boubou more amply about him.

"Well, young man, how are you?"

His hand enveloped Jean's in a pressure which was vigorous but not rough. The man was looking at the child, and his face, his beautiful face of shadow set in light, was all smiles for him. Jean had the impression that this man had known him forever, and that while he was smiling at him nothing else existed, nothing else had any importance.

"This is my son, Jean. He is not stupid, but he is very often on a trip to the moon."

That deplorable habit his father had of always divulging the family secrets! Jean would still have endured it, under all circumstances, but before this man!

"Sh . . . Don't make this big young man blush. I am sure that his journeys to the moon are thrilling—aren't they?"

Jean's confusion would have known no bounds if at this moment his attention had not been distracted by two light but firm raps on the door. Samba Diallo appeared. Jean's confusion gave way to surprise. Wearing a long white caftan and white sandals, Samba Diallo entered the room with a graceful and silent step, and made his way first toward M. Lacroix, who smilingly held out his hand. Then, with his own hand open, he stepped up to Jean:

"How do you do, Jean?"

"How do you do, Samba Diallo?"

Their hands met. Then Samba Diallo turned away and greeted the knight in the dalmatic. Neither of them was smiling any longer; they merely looked each other in the eyes for the space of several seconds, then, with the same movement, moved aside, their faces lighted up anew.

"I see that these young people are already acquainted," M. Lacroix said.

"Samba Diallo is my son," added the knight. "Where have you met, then—if that is not an indiscreet question?"

His tone was ironic as he spoke the last words.

"We sit at the same table in M. N'Diaye's class," Samba Diallo replied, without taking his eyes off Jean.

"Only we have hardly had any opportunity to talk together, have we?"

Samba Diallo's ease of manner, since he came into the room, left no doubt in Jean's mind: the knight's son had already met M. Lacroix. But none of this had been allowed to be seen at the school.

Blushing, Jean confirmed the fact that they had never spoken with each other.

Samba Diallo began to talk to his father in a low voice. Jean took advantage of this to go over to M. Lacroix.

The two boys left the office at the same time. Without speaking, they made their way into the white marl roadway, bordered with red flowers, which led to the portal of the Résidence. Samba Diallo snipped off a flower and began to look closely at it. After a short time he held it out to Jean.

"See, Jean, how beautiful this flower is," he said. "It smells good."

He was silent for an instant, then he added, unexpectedly,

"But it is going to die."

His eyes had been sparkling, and his nostrils had quivered a little, when he said that the flower was beautiful. A moment later he was obviously sad.

"It is going to die because you plucked it," Jean ventured to say.

"Yes—and if I had not done that, look what would have happened to it."

He picked a dry and spiny pod and showed it to

Jean. Then, with a springlike motion, he turned clear around, threw the pod away, and turned back to Jean, smiling:

"You wouldn't like to come and take a walk with me?"

"I should like it very much," Jean answered.

They went away from the Résidence and took one of those long streets of white marl that furrow the red sand of the little town of L. They walked along for some time without speaking, and soon abandoned the white marl for the red sand, a broad stretch of which, surrounded by milky euphorbia, lay straight ahead of them. In the middle of it Samba Diallo stopped, sat down, then lay out flat on his back, his hands at the nape of his neck and his face to the sky. Jean seated himself.

The sun was setting in an immense sweep of sky. Its rays, which are golden at this time of the day, had been dyed purple in their passage through the clouds that were setting the west afire. Struck diagonally by the light, the red sand was like seething gold.

Samba Diallo's basalt countenance had purple reflections. Basalt? It was a face of basalt because, also, it was as if turned to stone. No muscle in it, now, was moving. In his eyes the sky showed red. Since he lay down on the ground had Samba Diallo become riveted to it? Had he ceased to live? Jean was frightened.

"Tell me, Samba Diallo," he ventured, "what is a Diallobé?"

He had spoken for the sake of saying something.

The enchantment was shattered. Samba Diallo burst out laughing.

"Ah, they have been talking to you about me. . . . A Diallobé. . . . Well, my family, the Dialloubé, belong to the Diallobé people. We come from the banks of a great river. Our country is also called the Diallobé. I am the only one from this country in M. N'Diaye's class. They take advantage of that to joke about me."

"If you are a Diallobé, why didn't you stay in the Diallobé country?"

"And you, why did you leave Pau?"

Jean was embarrassed. But Samba Diallo went on at once:

"This is where I live, it is where I live all the time. It is true that I should have preferred to stay in the country, but my father lives here."

"He is a big man, your father. He is a bigger man than mine."

"Yes, he is a very big man."

While they were talking twilight had fallen. The golden rays had thinned out a little, and the purple had turned to pink. Along their lower edges the clouds had become a frozen blue. The sun had disappeared, but already in the east the moon had risen, and it, too, shed a light. One could see that the ambiant light was made up of the paling rose from the sun, the milky whiteness from the moon, and also the peaceful penumbra of a night which was felt to be imminent.

"Excuse me, Jean," said Samba Diallo. "It is twilight, and I must pray."

He rose, turned toward the east, lifted his arms, with his hands open, and slowly let them fall. His voice echoed in the quiet air. Jean did not dare to walk around his companion in order to see his face, but it seemed to him that this voice was no longer his. Samba Diallo remained motionless. Nothing in him was alive except this voice, speaking in the twilight a language which Jean did not understand. Then his long white caftan—turned violet now by the evening light—was swept through by a kind of shiver, which grew more pronounced in measure as the voice was rising. The shiver became a tremor which shook his entire body, and the voice turned to a sob. To the east the sky was like an immense lilac-colored crystal.

Jean did not know how long he remained there, held fascinated by Samba Diallo weeping under the sky. He never knew how much time was consumed by this pathetic and beautiful death of the day. He only regained consciousness of his surroundings when he heard the sound of footsteps not far away. He raised his head and saw the knight of the dalmatic, who came toward him, smiling, and held out his hand to help him get up. Samba Diallo was crouched on the ground, his head lowered, his body still trembling. The knight knelt down, took his son by the shoulders, set him on his feet, and smiled at him. Through his tears Samba Diallo smiled back, a bright smile. With a fold of his boubou the knight wiped the boy's face, very tenderly.

They conducted Jean, in silence, back to the marl street, then they retraced their steps to go to their own home. In the moonlight the street had the white sheen of lilies. Jean had watched the two figures disappearing in the distance, holding each other by the hand, then, slowly, he had gone back to his own house.

That night, thinking of Samba Diallo, he was overcome by fear. But that happened very late, when everyone had retired and Jean was alone, in his bed. That twilight's violence and splendor were not the cause of Samba Diallo's tears. Why had he wept?

For a long time the little boy was haunted by the two faces, of the father and the son. They continued to obsess him, until the moment when he sank into sleep.

6

As Samba Diallo and his father walked down the long
road the boy remained silent, as did his father also.
They walked slowly, each holding the other's hand.
Samba Diallo's agitation had quieted down. At last he
spoke:

"Have you news of the teacher of the Diallobé?"

"The teacher of the Diallobé is in good health. He
says that you are not to worry about him. He thinks of
you. You must not cry any more. . . . You are a man
now."

"No, it isn't that. . . ."

It was not sadness that had made him weep,
that evening. He knew now that the teacher of the
Diallobé would not leave him, even after his death. Even
Old Rella, held to Coumba by nothing but a memory
—a fleshly love—continued to stir her daughter. When
the teacher's fragile body had disappeared, what would
remain of him would be more than a love and a memory. For the rest, the teacher was still living, and yet
Samba Diallo no longer knew what he looked like—that
ridiculous appearance of his!—except in a blurred
fashion, through memory. Nevertheless, the teacher
continued to keep him on guard and to be present to his
attention, as effectively as if he had been there, holding
the burning faggot. When the teacher died, what was

left of him would be more exacting than memory. Old
Rella, when she was living, had had nothing but her
love; when she died her body disappeared completely
and her love left a memory. The teacher, Samba Diallo
was thinking, has a body so fragile that already it
seemed to be scarcely there. But, in addition, he has
the Word, which is made of nothing corporeal, but
which endures. . . . which endures. He has the fire
which runs like flame through the disciples and sets
the hearth aglow. He has that restless concern which
had more force than his body has weight. The disap-
pearance of this body—could it negate all that?

Dead love leaves a memory—and dead fervor? And
restless concern? The teacher, who was richer than Old
Rella, would die less completely than she. Samba Diallo
knew that.

This evening, in this twilight that was so beautiful,
he had felt himself swept by a sudden exaltation while
he was praying, an exaltation such as he had formerly
felt when he was near the teacher.

He lived over in his mind the circumstances of his
departure from the Glowing Hearth.

Some time after the chief of the Diallobé had found
Samba Diallo peacefully asleep close to Old Rella's
grave in the cemetery, there had been a long private
meeting between the chief, the teacher, and the Most
Royal Lady. The little boy never knew what they said
to one another. Afterward, the chief had called him
into his presence and had announced to him that he
was going to go back to L., to be with his father. At the
moment, Samba Diallo's joy had been overwhelming;

he had begun at once to think of L., and of his parents, with extraordinary intensity.

"But before you leave, you are going to say good-bye to the teacher," the chief had added.

At this word, Samba Diallo had felt his heart rising in his throat and choking him. The teacher. . . . What it amounted to was that he was about to leave the teacher. That was what his departure for L. meant. He would not see the teacher any more. The teacher's voice reciting the Word. . . . The look of the teacher as he listened to the Word. Far from the teacher, there were indeed his father and mother, there was indeed the sweetness of his home in L. But at the teacher's side Samba Diallo had known something else, which he had learned to love. When he tried to envisage to himself what it was that kept him so attached to the teacher, in spite of his burning faggots and his cruelties, Samba Diallo saw nothing, except perhaps that the reasons for this attraction were not of the same order as those which made him love his father and mother and his home in L. These reasons belonged rather with the fascination which the mystery of Old Rella exercised over his mind. They must be of the same order as those which made him hate being reminded of the noble status of his family. Whatever they might be, these reasons had an imperious power.

"Well, well, you are crying?" said the chief. "Think of that, at your age! You are not pleased to be going back to L.? Come here. Come close to me."

The chief of the Diallobé had taken the little boy on his knee. He had dried his tears gently and tenderly with a fold of his boubou, as his father, later, had done.

"You know, Samba Diallo, the teacher is very well satisfied with you. Come, stop crying, that is finished. . . ."

The chief had dried still other tears, as he held the trembling body of his little cousin tight against his breast.

"You know—when you go to see the teacher you will take him Tourbillon. I have given the necessary instructions to have him ready."

Tourbillon was a magnificent Arab thoroughbred that belonged to the chief.

"You will not be afraid? You will not let yourself be unseated, will you? In any case there will be someone with you. Ah, in that connection, the Most Royal Lady has some presents for you. Come with me to see them."

And that had been an unpacking of a treasure chest! There had been boubous in rich colors, Turkish slippers, woven loin-cloths, all made especially for Samba Diallo by the best artisans among the Diallobé. Later in the afternoon the little boy, mounted on Tourbillon and accompanied by a servant who was holding the horse's bridle to restrain his mettlesome spirits, set out for the teacher's house.

When he came near it he dismounted, and walked the rest of the way. At the teacher's door he removed his Turkish slippers, took them in his hand, and went in.

The teacher was seated among his disciples, who formed a noisy circle around him. As soon as he saw Samba Diallo, he smiled at him, and got up to greet him.

Samba Diallo, overwhelmed, ran to him and obliged him to remain seated.

"You see, my son, I do not even know how to get up any longer. But how handsome you are! Lord, how handsome you are! Just let me look! Come, come, what is this? You are weeping? But let us see—we know you are courageous nevertheless. You never used to cry when I beat you. . . ."

The disciples were silent. Samba Diallo felt a little ashamed of having wept before them.

"Master, I have come to say goodbye to you," he stammered. "I am very sad."

Tears choked him anew. He pulled the fold of his boubou over his head.

"My cousin begs you," he managed to go on, "to do him the favor of accepting—" He pointed his finger toward Tourbillon.

"Heavens above! Your cousin is lavishing his benefactions upon me, and that is the truth! This horse is too beautiful! And I cannot make a draft horse of him." The teacher was silent for a moment. "No, this horse cannot be a draft horse," he said, again. "His head is too high. He is too beautiful. One cannot ask a thoroughbred to draw the plough. . . ."

Then he had the look of awaking from a deep meditation.

"So you are going back to L.? You will not forget the Word, will you, my son? You will never forget it?"

"Lord," the teacher had prayed in thought, "never forsake this child. May the smallest measure of

Thy sovereign authority not leave him, for even the smallest particle of time."

Then Samba Diallo had taken a heavy package from the hands of the servant who accompanied him; it contained all the presents which had been given to him. Turning back, he had handed it to the teacher.

"I should like to give this to the disciples who might want it," he said.

"We shall pray for you, my child," the teacher had replied.

Samba Diallo had been almost running as he left the Hearth. Behind him he had heard the teacher, in a stern voice, asking the disciples what they were waiting for, to continue with the intoning of the Word.

That evening, the Diallobé people learned that the teacher had made the director of the new school a present of a thoroughbred horse. "This engaging animal," the teacher assured him, "will be more in place at the new school than at the Glowing Hearth."

A few days after that, Samba Diallo had set out for L.

A letter had announced to the knight that the older members of the Diallobé family, the Most Royal Lady as well as the chief, had decided to send Samba Diallo back to him so that he might be enrolled in the new school.

What the knight felt when he received the letter was like a blow in his heart. So, the victory of the foreigners was complete! Here were the Diallobé, here was,

his own family, on their knees before a burst of fire-
works. A solar burst, it is true, the midday burst of an
exasperated civilization. The knight was suffering
deeply in the face of this irreparable thing which was
being accomplished here, before his eyes, upon his own
flesh. Those who, even down to his own family, who
were racing headlong into the future, if they could only
understand that their course was a suicide, their sun a
mirage! If only he himself were of the stature to rise up
before them on their road, and put an end to that blind
contest!

"In truth, it is not acceleration which the world
needs," the knight reflected. "What we must have is a
bed, a bed upon which, stretched out, the soul will de-
termine a respite, in the name of its salvation. Is civilization outside the balance of man and his disposability?
The civilized man, is he not the expendable man—expendable for the love of his fellows, expendable above
all for the love of God? But, a voice within him will object, man is surrounded by problems which prevent
this quietude. He is born to a forest of questions. The
substance of matter in which he participates through
his body—which the soul hates—harasses him with a
cacophony of demands to which he must respond. 'I am
hungry. Give me something to eat,' his stomach orders.
'Are we going to rest at last? Let us rest,' his limbs keep
murmuring. To his stomach and his limbs, a man gives
the answers that are called for; and this man is happy.
Then a voice implores him: 'I am alone. I am afraid
to be alone. I am not sufficient in loneliness. Find me
someone to love.' And this voice, particularly plaintive,

lamenting day and night: 'I am afraid. I am afraid. What is my native country? Who brought me here? Where are they taking me?' The man rises and goes in search of man. Then he isolates himself and prays. This man is at peace. Man must respond to all the questions. You, you wish to ignore some of them. . . . No," the knight objected for his own part, "no, I only wish for harmony. The most strident voices try to drown out the others. Is that good? Civilization is an architecture of responses. Its perfection, like that of any dwelling house, is measured by the comfort man feels in it, by the added portion of liberty it procures for him. But, precisely, the Diallobé are not free—and you would like to maintain this condition? No, that is not what I want. But man's slavery amid a forest of solutions—is that worth anything more?"

The knight was turning these thoughts over and over in his mind, in a thousand ways.

"Happiness is not a function of the mass of responses, but of their distribution. There must be balance. But the West is possessed by its own compulsion, and the world is becoming westernized. Far from men's resisting the madness of the West at the time when they ought to do so, in order to pick and choose, assimilate or reject, we see them, on the contrary, in all latitudes, a-quiver with covetousness, then metamorphosing themselves in the space of one generation, under the action of this new egotism which the West is scattering abroad."

At this point in his reflections the knight had something like an hallucination. A spot on our globe was burning with a blinding brilliance, as if a fire had been lighted on an immense hearth. At the heart of this fierce light and heat a swarm of human beings seemed to be giving themselves over to an incomprehensible and fantastic mimicry of worship. Emerging from all sides, from deep valleys of shadow, floods of human creatures of all colors were pouring in; and in the measure of their approach to the hearth, these beings took up, insensibly, the rhythm which encompassed them, while under the effect of the light they lost their original colors, which gave way to the wan tint that filled the air roundabout.

The knight closed his eyes to banish the vision. To live in the shadow, to live humbly and peaceably at the obscure heart of the world, to live from his own substance and his own wisdom. . . .

So when he had received the letter from the chief of the Diallobé the knight had remained seated for a long time. Then he had got up, gone to a corner of the courtyard, turned his face toward the east, and prayed long and earnestly to his Lord. Samba Diallo would go to the school, if such was the will of God.

He had refrained from any sort of outburst at the time of the boy's return. But through his calm and his affectionate solicitude Samba Diallo had perceived profound grief. In the face of this disapproval which was not expressed, this sadness by which the knight was not crushed, in the face of this silence of his father's, Samba Diallo had melted into tears, and a thousand times regretted his departure from the Glowing Hearth.

On that first night, it would seem that Nature had wished to associate itself with a delicate thought of the

boy's, for the luminous twilight had scarcely died away
when a thousand stars had sprung forth in the sky. The
moon was born at the heart of their scintillating festival,
and a mystic exaltation seemed suddenly to fill the
night.

The house was silent. The knight, stretched out on
a chaise longue on the veranda, was absorbed in meditation. The women, grouped around the mother of the
family, were talking in very low tones.

Samba Diallo quietly left his room on the court,
walked up and down and across, and then, slowly,
recited the prelude to the Night of the Koran,* which
he offered to the knight. His voice, scarcely audible at
first, gradually rose and grew stronger. Progressively,
he felt that an emotion was sweeping through him in an
experience he had never had before. Every word had
ceased, throughout the house. The knight, at first lying
down indifferent to what was going on about him, had
stood up when he heard the voice of Samba Diallo, and
it seemed now that in listening to the Word he sustained
the same levitation as that which increased the teacher's
stature. Samba Diallo's mother had detached herself
from the group of women and come close to her son.
From feeling himself listened to, so, by the two beings
whom he loved the most, from knowing that on this en-
chanted night he, Samba Diallo, was repeating for his
father what the knight himself had repeated for his
own father, what from generation to generation through

* It was the custom that the child who had completed his studies in
the Koran and returned to his parents should, in their honor, recite
the Holy Book from memory throughout all of one night.

centuries the sons of the Diallobé had repeated for their fathers, from knowing that he had not failed in this respect and that he was about to prove to all who were listening that the Diallobé would not die in him—from all this, there was a moment when Samba Diallo was on the point of fainting. But he considered that it was important for him, more than for any of those who had preceded him, to acquit himself to the full on his Night. For it seemed to him that this Night marked an end. This scintillation of the heavens above his head, was it not the star-studded bolt being drawn upon an epoch that had run its course? Behind that bolt a world of stellar light was gently glowing, a world which it was important to glorify one last time. His voice, which had progressively risen as if linked to the thrust of the stars, was raised now to a pathetic fullness. From the depths of the ages he felt, springing up in him and breathed out by his voice, a long love which today was threatened. In the humming sound of this voice there was being dissolved, bit by bit, a being who a few moments ago had still been Samba Diallo. Insensibly, rising from profundities which he did not suspect, phantoms were assailing him through and through and were substituting themselves for him. It seemed to him that in his voice had become muffled innumerable voices, like the voice of the river on certain nights.

But the voice of the river was less vehement, and also less close to tears. The voice of the river did not carry along with it this refusal which was now being cried out in the voice of Samba Diallo; nor did it have the accompaniment of this nostalgic chant.

For a long time, in the night, his voice was that of the voiceless phantoms of his ancestors, whom he had raised up. With them, he wept their death; but also, in long cadence, they sang his birth.

7

On the horizon, it seemed as if the earth were poised on the edge of an abyss. Above the abyss the sun was suspended, dangerously. The liquid silver of its heat had been reabsorbed, without any loss of its light's splendor. Only, the air was tinted with red, and under this illumination the little town seemed suddenly to belong to a strange planet.

Behind his closed window, Paul Lacroix stood waiting. Waiting for what? The whole town was waiting too, in the same dismayed expectation. The man's gaze wandered over the sky, where long lines of red rays were joining the sun, dying at a zenith invaded by invidious shade. "They are right," he thought, "I really believe that this is the moment. The world is about to come to an end. The moment is fragile. It may break. Then, time will be blocked off. No!" Paul Lacroix stopped short of articulating this No. With a brusque gesture he pulled the green curtain that hung above the window down over the reddened glass. The office took on the appearance of a bluish-green aquarium. Paul Lacroix made his way slowly back to his chair.

At his desk, Samba Diallo's father had remained motionless, as if indifferent to the cosmic drama being played out outside. His white boubou had turned to violet. Its broad folds helped by their immobility to give him the appearance of a figure of stone. "Jean is right," Lacroix thought. "He has the air of a knight of the Middle Ages."

He turned and spoke to him:

"Does this twilight not trouble you? Myself, I am upset by it. At this moment it seems to me that we are closer to the end of the world than we are to nightfall."

The knight smiled.

"Reassure yourself. I predict for you a peaceful night."

"You do not believe in the end of the world?"

"On the contrary, I even hope for it, firmly."

"That is just what I was thinking. Here everyone believes in the end of the world, from the most simple-minded peasant to the man of great cultivation. Why? I have been asking myself; and only today, with this twilight, I have begun to understand."

The knight looked attentively at Paul.

"Let me ask you a question in my turn: you truly do not believe in the end of the world?"

"No, obviously. The world will not come to an end —at least not to the end that is expected here. That a catastrophe might destroy our planet—of that I do not speak."

"Our most simple-minded peasant does not believe in such an end as that, episodic and accidental. His universe does not admit of accident. In spite of appearances, his concept is more reassuring than yours."

"That may well be. Unfortunately for us, it is my universe which is true. The earth is not flat. It has no steep slopes which give upon the abyss. The sun is not a candelabrum set upon a blue porcelain dais. The universe which science has revealed to the West is less immediately human, but confess that it is more solid."

"Your science has revealed to you a round and perfect world, in infinite movement," said the knight. "It has reconquered that world from chaos. But I believe that in so doing it has laid you open to despair."

"Not at all. It has liberated us from fears—childish and absurd fears."

"Absurd? What is absurd is the world which does not end. When will one know the truth—all the truth? As for us, we still believe in the coming of truth. We hope for it."

Then that is it, Paul Lacroix thought. The truth which they do not now possess, which they are incapable of conquering, they hope for in the end. It is so in the case of justice, also. All they want and do not have —instead of trying to conquer it, they await it at the end. . . .

He did not express this thought. He merely said:

"As for us, we conquer a little more of truth each day, thanks to science. We do not wait. . . ."

I was sure that he would not have understood, thought the knight. They are so fascinated by the returns they get from the implement that they have lost sight of the infinite immensity of the workyard. They do not see that the truth which they discover each day is each day more contracted. A little truth each day—to be sure, that must be, that is necessary. But the Truth? To have *this*, must one renounce *that?*

Like Paul Lacroix, he did not express this thought aloud. He said, instead:

"I believe that you understand very well what I want to say to you. I do not contest the quality of the truth which science discloses. But it is a partial truth; and insofar as there will be a future, all truth will be partial. Truth takes its place at the end of history. But I see that we are setting out on the deceptive road of metaphysics."

"Why do you say 'deceptive'?"

" 'To every word one can oppose another'—is that not what one of your ancient philosophers has said? Tell me frankly if this is not still your conviction to-day."

"No. And, if you please, let us keep away from metaphysics. I should like to know your world."

"You know it already. Our world is that which believes in the end of the world: which at the same time hopes for it and fears it. Just now, I rejoiced greatly when it seemed to me that you were in anguish there in front of the window. See, I was saying to myself, he has a foreboding of the end. . . ."

"No, it was not anguish, truly. It did not go so far as that."

"Then from the bottom of my heart I wish for you to rediscover the feeling of anguish in the face of the dying sun. I ardently wish that for the West. When the sun dies, no scientific certainty should keep us from weeping for it, no rational evidence should keep us from asking that it be reborn. You are slowly dying

under the weight of evidence. I wish you that anguish—
like a resurrection."

"To what shall we be born?"

"To a more profound truth. Evidence is a quality
of the surface. Your science is the triumph of evidence,
a proliferation of the surface. It makes you the masters
of the external, but at the same time it exiles you there,
more and more."

There was a moment of silence. Outside, the ves-
peral drama had come to an end. The sun had set. Behind it, an imposing mass of bright red cloud had come
crumbling down like a monstrous stream of clotted
blood. The red splendor of the air had been progressively softened under the impact of the slow invasion of
the evening shade.

Strange, Lacroix was thinking, this fascination of
nothingness for those who have nothing. Their nothingness—they call it the absolute. They turn their backs to
the light, but they look at the shadow fixedly. Is it that
this man is not conscious of his poverty?

The knight's voice broke the silence now, but in a
low and meditative tone, as if he were speaking to himself:

"I should like to say to you, nevertheless—" he
hesitated.

"What do you wish to say, Monsieur?"

"I should like to tell you that it is myself, ultimately,
who have sent my son to your school."

"It is your turn to make me very happy," Paul
Lacroix said.

"I have sent my son to your school, and I have prayed God to save us all, you and us."

"He will save us, if He exists."

"I have sent my son to the school because the external which you have checked was slowly seeping through us and destroying us. Teach him to check the external."

"We have checked it."

"The external is aggressive. If man does not conquer it, then it destroys man, and makes him a victim of tragedy. A sore which is neglected does not heal, but becomes infected to the point of gangrene. A child who is not educated goes backward. A society which is not governed destroys itself. The West sets up science against the invading chaos, sets it up like a barricade."

At this moment Lacroix had to fight against the strong temptation to push the electric light switch which was within reach of his hand. He would have liked to scrutinize the shadowed face of this motionless man who sat opposite him. In his voice he perceived a tonality which intrigued him, and which he would have liked to relate to the expression of his face. But, No, he thought, if I turn on the light this man may stop talking. It is not to me that he is talking, it is to himself. He listened.

"Every hour that passes brings a supplement of ignition to the crucible in which the world is being fused. We have not had the same past, you and ourselves, but we shall have, strictly, the same future. The era of separate destinies has run its course. In that sense, the end of the world has indeed come for every one of us, because no one can any longer live by the simple carrying out of what he himself is. But from our long and varied ripenings a son will be born to the world: the first son of the earth; the only one, also."

In the darkness Lacroix felt that the knight was turning slightly toward him.

"M. Lacroix, this future—I accept it," he said. "My son is the pledge of that. He will contribute to its building. It is my wish that he contribute, not as a stranger come from distant regions, but as an artisan responsible for the destinies of the citadel."

"He will teach us the secrets of the shade. He will reveal to us the springs at which your youth quenches its thirst."

"Do not do violence to yourself, M. Lacroix! I know that you do not believe in the shade; nor in the end of the world. What you do not see does not exist. The moment, like a raft, carries you on the luminous surface of its round disc, and you deny the abyss that lies about you. The future citadel, thanks to my son, will open its wide windows on the abyss, from which will come great gusts of shadow upon our shrivelled bodies, our haggard brows. With all my soul I wish for this opening. In the city which is being born such should be our work—all of us, Hindus, Chinese, South Americans, Negroes, Arabs, all of us, awkward and pitiful, we the under-developed, who feel ourselves to be clumsy in a world of perfect mechanical adjustment."

It was becoming quite dark now. Lacroix, not moving, heard in the shadow this strange prayer:

"God in Whom I believe, if we are not to succeed, let the Apocalypse come! Take away from us that liberty of which we shall not have known how to make use. May Thy hand fall heavily, then, upon the great unconsciousness. May the arbitrary power of Thy will throw out of order the stable course of our laws. . . ."

8

"Why should they wish me to know?" the teacher was thinking. "They know better than I do what it is that they want. At bottom—"

He interrupted himself to scratch energetically at his side. Raising the fold of his boubou he saw a fat brown bug running over his skin. He picked it up, delicately, and set it on the ground, then he went back to his bed.

"At bottom, they have already chosen. They are like a woman who consents to intercourse: the child that is not yet conceived is calling to her; it must be that the child shall be born. This country awaits a child. But in order that the child may be born the country must give itself. . . . And that—that . . . But also, in the long run, would dire poverty not fill our hearts with bitterness? Dire poverty is the enemy of God. . . ."

The teacher's whole right side was hurting him. He turned over on his back.

Nothing in the teacher's house, this day, had risen toward heaven—neither the flame of the hearth nor the echo of young voices. The teacher had reduced his prayers to the strict minimum. He who used to sleep little because he was always praying had remained in bed since morning, and his body, unaccustomed to such soft treatment, was fatigued by this repose.

Upon this silent house, however, was concentrated the thought of the entire country of the Diallobé: upon this house and the unquiet form which it held in its bosom, like the almond enclosed in its shell.

The teacher could have said Yes—that was easy —and the country would have exploded with joy. It would have been easy for him to say No, and the country would have obeyed him. He was saying nothing. The men of the Diallobé sensed the drama that was going on within him, and thought of their teacher both gratefully and with compassion.

"My God," he prayed, "Thou hast willed that Thy creatures should live on the solid shell of appearance. Truth would drown them. But, Lord of truth, Thou knowest that appearance proliferates and hardens. Lord, preserve us from exile behind appearance."

It was on the evening before that the delegation had come. They were led by Ardo Diallobé, first son of the country. Also to be noticed among them were Dialtobé, the master of the fishermen, Farba, the teacher of the griots,* the chief of the guild of smiths, that of the guild of shoemakers, and many besides. The teacher's house had been filled to overflowing.

"Master," Ardo Diallobé had told him, "the country will do what you say."

"I will say nothing," the teacher had replied, "be-

* The griots are, in certain African countries, a special class of musicians, poets, historians, sorcerers, and the like. Tr.

cause I know nothing. I am only the humble guide for your children, and not at all for you, my brothers."

A silence had followed this, and then the first son of the Diallobé had taken up the plea again:

"The Word, certainly, can suspend itself like a garment, master. Life does not suspend itself. The time has come for our country to reach a decision. The chief of the Diallobé has said to us, 'I am the hand which acts. It is you, people of the Diallobé, who are the body and the brain. Speak, and I shall act.' What shall we say?"

The teacher, then, had stood up.

"I swear upon the Word that I do not know. What a man really knows is for him like the succession of numbers: he can say it over indefinitely, and take it in all senses, going on without limits. What I could say to you, on the contrary, is short and plain: 'Act,' or, again, 'Do not act.' Nothing more. Do you not see for yourselves how easily that can be said, and how there is no more reason to say *this* than *that?*"

The teacher had spoken with vehemence, and he was looking at all of them at the same time, as if to communicate to each of them the conviction that he knew nothing. But they had remained gloomy. Perhaps the teacher had spoken in words that were too lofty. As he returned to the subject now, he was seeking to explain himself in another way:

"People of the Diallobé, I know what you are waiting for. You do not know what you ought to do. And so you have thought, Let us go to see the teacher of our children, so that he may tell us what we ought to do. . . . Isn't that it?"

"Exactly," the first son of the Diallobé agreed.

"You are waiting for me to indicate to you what you ought to do, as ten indicates the following eleven to the man who can count. Isn't that so?" the teacher went on.

There was a murmur of acquiescence.

"People of the Diallobé, I swear to you that I have no such knowledge as that. As much as yourselves, I should like to know. . . ."

The men who were gathered there looked at one another in deep uncertainty and dismay. If the teacher did not know, then who would know? The country must reach a decision nevertheless. Travelers coming from distant provinces were reporting that men everywhere had chosen to send their children to the foreign school. These new generations were going to learn how to build dwelling houses, how to care for the bodies within those dwelling houses, as the foreigners knew how to do.

The teacher did not notice when his guests left him. Having spoken, he had become lost in his thoughts once more.

When the fool came, he found the teacher in the same position, lying straight out on his back, one arm along his side, the other folded over his face, above his eyes.

The man who thus arrived was belted into an old frock-coat, under which the least movement he made revealed that he was wearing the ample garments of the Diallobé. The age of the frock-coat, and its doubtful cleanliness over the immaculate neatness of the boubous, bestowed an unusual appearance upon this personage. His physiognomy, like his clothes, left an impression of strangeness. Its features were immobile and impassive, except for the eyes, which were never quiet for an instant. One might have said that the man knew a secret which was baleful to the world, and which he was forcing himself by a constant effort to keep from springing to his lips. The inconstancy of his ever-roving glance, the changing expressions of which died almost before they were born, raised a doubt, after the first impression, as to whether this man's brain could contain a single lucid thought.

He spoke little—and that was since people had begun to call him "the fool."

This man, who was an authentic son of the countryside, had left home some time before, without even his family knowing where he was going. He had been absent for a number of years, then one morning he had suddenly turned up, buttoned into his frock-coat. At the time of his return he had been very loquacious: he claimed that he had come back from the white man's country, and that he had fought against the white men there. At first he was taken at his word, though none of the other sons of the countryside who had been in this white men's war said that they had ever seen him. But, fairly soon, people began to doubt his recitals.

In the first place, this was because his story was so

extravagant that it was difficult to put any faith in it. But even more than the extravagance of the narrative itself, it was the man's histrionic art that worried them. In measure as he recounted events, the fool would begin to relive, as if in a frenzy, the circumstances of his recital. One day, in explaining how he had been wounded in the abdomen—in fact he did have a scar there—the man had suddenly crumpled up, then fallen, his arms on his abdomen, while a rattle of agony came from his throat. After that, his fellows had taken pains to avoid him, while he himself would recover from his crises only to go in search of indulgent listeners, before whom he would bring the events of his memories dramatically to life.

One day he found out that he had been nicknamed "the fool." Upon that he relapsed into silence. But the nickname clung to him nevertheless.

Now, the man sat down beside the teacher, whom he believed to be asleep, in order to wait for him to wake up.

"Oh, it is you?" the teacher said as he opened his eyes. "What are you doing there?"

"They are tiring you very much, aren't they—all these people?"

And the fool pointed vaguely to the houses around the teacher's dwelling.

"Chase them away," he added. "You will chase them away, won't you, the next time they come?"

For the fraction of a second his burning glance had the look of one waiting anxiously for a reply.

"Tell me, you will chase them away, won't you?"

"Yes," the teacher agreed, "I will chase them away."

The other man quieted down.

"Now they are coming to you," he said. "They are humble and gentle, like sheep. But you must not deceive yourself. At bottom, they are not sheep. It is because you are still there, with your empty house and your poor garments, that they still remain sheep. But you are going to die, you and your poor house also. Then speedily their nature will change; I tell you, from the time of your dying. It is only your survival that delays the metamorphosis."

He leaned down and, with passion, kissed the teacher's hand. The latter sprang up, pulled back his hand as if it had been burnt, then, changing his mind, held it out to the fool, who began to caress it.

"You see, when you die," the fool said, "all these houses of straw will die with you. Everything here will be as it is down there—you know, down there. . . ."

The teacher, who had gone back to lying down, wished to get up, but the fool, gently, held him back. He simply drew a little closer to him, and delicately raising his head from the floor he placed it comfortably against the fleshy part of his thigh.

"How is it, down there?" the teacher asked.

A furtive expression of happiness came over the fool's face.

"Truly? You want me to tell you?"

"Yes, tell me."

So the fool spoke:

"It was morning when I disembarked there. From

my first steps in the street I felt an unspeakable anguish. It seemed to me that my heart and my body were contracting, together. I shivered, and I came back to the enormous debarcation hall. My legs were soft and trembling under me. I had a great desire to sit down. Around me, the stone floor was spread out like a brilliant mirror of sound that echoed the clattering of men's shoes. At the centre of the immense hall I noticed an agglomeration of upholstered armchairs. But my eyes had hardly fallen upon them when I felt a return of that nervous twitching, as if my whole body were in exaggerated revolt. I set my valises on the floor and sat down right on the cold stone. Passers-by paused around me. A woman came up to me. She spoke to me. I thought I understood that she was asking me if I felt all right. The agitation of my body quieted down, in spite of the cold of the pavement, which penetrated my very bones. I spread out my hands, flat, on this icy tiling. I even was seized with a desire to take off my shoes, to touch with my feet that cold glaucous brilliant mirror. But I was vaguely conscious of an incongruity. I merely stretched out my legs, which came in contact all along their length, so, with the frozen floor."

The teacher raised himself slightly to look into the fool's eyes. He had been struck by the unexpected coherence of this recital. His surprise increased when he saw that the fool's gaze was now fixed. He had never seen him like this. The teacher laid his head again on the man's knees and felt that he was trembling slightly.

The fool went on:

"Already a little group had formed around me. A man cleared a way to me and took hold of my wrist. Then he made a sign that I was to be put on a nearby sofa. When eager hands were held out to lift me from the floor I pushed them aside and with a free movement of my own I got up, towering by a head above all of them. I had recovered my serenity, and now that I was standing up all they could see of me was that I was solidly built and perfectly healthy. Around me, I sensed that the people were consulting with one another, a little surprised at my sudden resurrection. I stammered some words of apology. Then I bent down and, easily picking up a heavy valise in each hand, I walked through the circle of flabbergasted spectators. But no sooner had I got into the street than I felt that nervous twitching attacking me again. At the cost of considerable effort I kept anything from being seen, and I hurried away from that place. At my back I felt the weight of many eyes fixed upon me, through the windows of the immense hall. I turned a corner of the street and catching sight of a door set deep in a wall, I put my valises on the ground and sat down on one of them, sheltered from the solicitude of passers-by. It was high time, for my trembling was beginning again to become apparent. What I felt went deeper than the mere revolt of my body. This trembling, which was again subsiding now that I was sitting down, seemed to me to be my body's fraternal echo to an inward disturbance. A man passing by me seemed to want to stop. I turned my head away. The man hesitated, then shook his own head and went on. I followed him with my eyes: his square back was lost among other square backs, his grey gabardine lost among other gabardines; the dry clatter of his shoes was mingled with the sound as of castanets that ran along the level of the asphalt. The asphalt. . . . My gaze traversed the entire extent of what lay before me, and I saw no limit to the stony surface: down there, the icy feldspar, here the light grey of the stone, the dull black of the asphalt; nowhere the tender softness of the bare earth.

"On the hard asphalt, my exacerbated ears and my eager eyes were vainly on the look-out for the soft upheaval of earth from a naked foot. There was no foot anywhere around me. On the hard carapace, there was only the clattering of a thousand hard shells. Had men no longer feet of flesh? A woman passed me, the pink flesh of her calves hardened monstrously in two black terminal conches at the level of the asphalt. I had not seen one single human foot since I disembarked. All along the asphalt, the tide of shells ran level with it. All around, from the pavement to the house rooftops, the bare and echoing shell of the stone turned the street into a basin of granite. This valley of stone was traversed on its axis by a fantastic river of wild and head-strong mechanisms. Never to this day had the automobiles—which I nevertheless knew—seemed to me so sovereign and so mad, so crafty, though still obedient. On the height of paved street that they held, there was not one human being walking. Never had I seen that, teacher of the Diallobé. There before me, in a built-up and inhabited area, along great lengths of roadway, it was given to me to contemplate an expanse that was completely dehumanized, empty of men. Imagine that, master, in the very heart of the city of men, an expanse forbidden to his naked flesh, forbidden to the alternating contacts of his two feet. . . ."

"Is that true?" the teacher broke in. "Is it true that at the heart of his own dwelling place the furtive form of man should now know spaces fatal to him?"

The fool trembled with joy over having been so well understood.

"Yes, I have seen it. You know, master, the delicate silhouette which rests on one leg then on the other, in order to advance?"

"Yes. And then?"

"In man's own dwelling place I have seen these deadly spaces. Mechanisms are reigning there."

The fool fell silent. Both men remained silent for a long time. Then the teacher asked, gently,

"What else have you seen?"

"Truly? You want me to tell you?"

"Yes, tell me."

"I have seen the mechanisms. They are shells. It is a rolled-up expanse, which moves. Well, you know that expanse has nothing inside it; therefore it has nothing to lose. It cannot be wounded, like the form of man, but only unrolled. Also, it has forced back man's form, fearful that it, in being wounded, will lose the internal substance it contains."

"I understand you. Go on."

"This expanse moves. Well, you know it was stability itself which made the movement apparent, like its mirror. Now it has begun to move. Its movement is more finished than the progressive jerkings of man's hesitant form. It cannot fall—where would it fall to? Also, it has forced back the silhouette of man, which is afraid, in falling, of losing movement."

Again the fool fell silent. The teacher, supporting himself on his elbow, got up and saw that his visitor was weeping.

The teacher sat down, drew the fool to him, and made him lean against his breast, the fool's head in the hollow of the teacher's shoulder. He dried the man's tears with his bare hand, then, gently, began to rock him to and fro.

"Master, I should like to pray with you," the fool said, "to repel the upheaval. There is obscene chaos in the world once more, and it defies us."

9

The knight took off his eyeglasses, closed his Koran, and for some time remained motionless, with his face to the east. His countenance was at once grave and serene. Samba Diallo, lying on a rug near him, slipped the pencil from his right hand between the pages of the book he was reading, and looked at his father.

"The Word must continue to echo within him," the boy said to himself. "He is one of those who do not cease to pray when they have closed their prayer book. To him, God is a constant Presence—constant and indispensable. It is this Presence, I believe, which stretches the skin tight across the bones of his forehead, and sets that luminous and profound expression within the deep-cut orbits of his eyes. His mouth holds no smile, nor does it hold any bitterness. All the profane exuberance of life must certainly be burned out of this man by his profound prayers. My father does not live, he prays . . .

"But wait a minute! Why did I think that?" he caught himself up. "Why did I think of prayer and life in terms of opposition? He prays, he does not live. . . . Certainly no one else in this house would have thought that way. I am the only one who could have this bizarre idea of a life which could be lived, in some fashion, outside the presence of God. . . . Curious. Bizarre idea. Then where could I have got it? This idea is foreign to me. The astonishment into which it plunges me is proof of that. It is, in any case, an idea that has evolved. I mean to say, an idea that marks a progress in precision over my previous state of mind: it distinguishes; it specifies. There is God and there is life, two things not necessarily intermingled. There is prayer and there is combat. Is this idea right? If I listened to that man sleeping more and more profoundly within me, I should reply, No, this idea is even mad; life is only of a secondary order: it is from time to time. God alone is, continually, uninterruptedly. Life is only in the measure and of the fashioning of the being of God.

"So this man within me would say; would he be right? Evil is of life; is evil of God? There is something even more simple and prosaic; let us take work. I cannot struggle, work, to live and support my family, and at the same time be fully with God. My teacher at the Glowing Hearth prays all the time, except when he is busy cultivating the soil—and even then, to be sure, he is still chanting litanies. But he does not pray in the same way as when he is before the hearth, on his prayer rug. So it is with my father. With him, the case is even more clear. When he is in his office, he is less close to God than the teacher is in the fields. My father's work absorbs his thought. Carried to its limit, a work in which a man was completely absorbed would keep him all the time outside God. There is no work, it is true, which completely absorbs the man who is engaged in it. But there are countries where great masses

of men have long been alienated from God. Perhaps.
. . . Perhaps it is work which makes the West more
and more atheistic. . . . A curious idea. . . ."

"What are you reading?"

Still seated on his rug, the knight was smiling at
his son, in a pause in his prayer.

Samba Diallo held out the book he was still holding in his hand.

"*Les Pensées*. . . . Hmm. . . . Pascal. Of the
men of the West, he is certainly the most reassuring.
But be distrustful even of him. He had doubted. Exile
had known him too. It is true that he came back afterward, running. He wept, sobbing, over having gone
astray, and he called upon the 'God of Abraham, Isaac,
and Jacob' against that of 'the philosophers and scholars.' The road of his return began like a miracle and
ended like an act of grace. The men of the West know
less and less of the miracle and the act of grace. . . ."

"But just then I was thinking that perhaps it is because the West works—"

"What do you mean to say? I don't know if I understand your objection."

Samba Diallo did not dare to reveal to his father
the whole tenor of his thought, and in particular the
formidable break which he had believed he discovered.
In considering how much he himself had been surprised, he was afraid of worrying him. He tempered his
words, therefore:

"You have spoken of Pascal's exile, thinking no
doubt of that part of his life which preceded the

Mémorial. . . . Now this period of dereliction was also a period of intense scientific toil. . . ."

"Yes, I understand you. But your idea is bizarre."

The knight regarded his son in silence for several seconds. Then, instead of answering his implied question, he asked,

"Why, in your opinion, does one work?"

"In order to live."

"Your answer pleases me. But in your place I should have been less categorical. My reply would have been enumerative, in the following form, for example: 'One can work to live, one can work to outlive, so to speak, in the hope of multiplying the life one has, if not in its duration—one cannot do that as yet—at least in its intensity. The aim of work is then accumulation. One can work—in order to work; that happens.' My enumeration is not restrictive. Do you admit that I am more in the way of truth than you are, and that my enumeration is just?"

"Yes."

The knight clasped his beautiful hands over his knees. His gaze was lost in the distance before him. "Even while he thinks, he has the air of one praying," Samba Diallo said to himself. "Perhaps he is really praying? God has indeed entered into his entire being."

"Therefore," the knight went on, "one may work from necessity, for the cessation of the great pain of need which wells up from the body and from the earth —to impose silence on all those voices which harass us with their demands. Then, too, one works to maintain oneself, to preserve the species. But one can also work from greed. In this case, one is not trying to block off the pit of need; that has been wholly filled already. One is not even seeking to defer the next date when that need's claims will come due. One accumulates frantically, believing that in multiplying riches one multiplies life. Finally, one can work from a mania for working—I do not say to distract oneself, it is more frenzied than that; one works like a stereotype. It is with work as with the sexual act: both are aimed at the perpetuation of the species; but both may have their perversion when they do not justify themselves by this aim."

His gaze, which had been far off, seemed now to come closer. He changed his position and leaned toward Samba Diallo. "Oh, how handsome he is!" he was thinking, "And how I love him for being so impassioned over his idea!" He asked,

"Would you like us now to enlarge upon and examine these ideas in relation to God?"

"Yes. Let us take the case where work is aimed at the preservation of life. Let us reason about that, since it is the case of necessity. Even in this case work diminishes the place of God in the attention of man. There is a reason why this idea offends me: it seems to me contradictory. The conservation of life—thus the labor which makes it possible—ought to be a work of piety. The contemplation of God is the work of piety *par excellence*. Whence comes the clash of these two aims, which are nevertheless in other ways the same?"

All the time he was talking, Samba Diallo had kept

his eyes lowered, partly to follow out his idea better and partly to escape the knight's gaze. When he had finished speaking he raised his eyes again. The knight, still in the same posture of prayer, was now smiling, with an air at once delighted and mocking. His eyes were gleaming. "He is sparkling, the monk is sparkling," Samba Diallo thought.

"Why do you so stubbornly keep your eyes on the floor? Let us rather discuss together, apprentice philosopher," his father said. He lost his sparkling expression as he continued, after a short pause: "I prefer the ideas that are tried out in the full light of day to those that are allowed to grow rancid within oneself. It is these last that poison, and sometimes kill."

He recovered his serenity on the instant and began to smile again.

"To come back to the idea that is worrying you— it seems to me, my young philosopher, that we ought to get a better hold on it, to get it pure and simple, so to speak. Now the idea of work for the preservation of life does not appear to me as sufficiently simple. It has anterior stages."

"Certainly: for example, the very idea of life, insofar as it has value."

"Bravo! Let us consider work in the case where it is linked to life by a relation of justification. I say that everything which justifies life and gives it its meaning, in the same way and *a posteriori*, gives work its meaning, too."

"I see your conclusion," Samba Diallo said. "When a life justifies itself before God, everything that tends to preserve it—hence, work—is also justified in His eyes."

"Correct. Work, in effect, is justified before God in strict measure as the life it preserves justifies itself before Him. If a man believes in God, the time he takes from prayer for work is still prayer. It is even a very beautiful prayer."

Samba Diallo was silent for a long time. The knight was absorbed in his thoughts. He was no longer smiling.

"I add—but this is no more than the expression of a personal conviction—that a life which justifies itself before God would not know how to love exuberance, superabundance. It finds its full flowering, on the contrary, in the consciousness it has of its own littleness compared to the greatness of God. As it goes on its way it becomes larger, but that is of no importance to it."

"But if the life does not justify itself before God?" the boy asked. "I mean to say, if the man who is working does not believe in God?"

"Then what does it matter to him to justify his work in any other way than by the profit he gets from it? Life in this case is not a work of piety. Life is life, short as that may seem to you."

They were silent again for some time. Then the knight spoke once more:

"The West is in process of overturning these simple ideas, of which we are part and parcel. They began, timidly, by relegating God to a place 'between inverted commas.' Then two centuries later, having acquired more assurance, they decreed, 'God is dead.' From that day dates the era of frenzied toil. Nietzsche is the contemporary of the industrial revolution. God was no longer there to measure and justify man's activity. Was it not industry that did that? Industry was blind, although, finally, it was still possible to domicile all the good it produced. . . . But already this phase is past. . . . After the death of God, what they are now announcing is the death of man."

"I do not understand," Samba Diallo said.

"Life and work are no longer commensurable. In former times there existed a sort of iron law which decreed, in action, that the labor of one single life was able to provide for only one single life. Man's art has destroyed this law. The work of a single being supplies nourishment for several others, for more and more persons. But now see: the West is on the point of being able to do without man in the production of work. There will no longer be need of more than a very little life to furnish an immense amount of labor."

"But it seems to me," the boy objected, "that we ought to rejoice in this prospect instead of regretting it."

"No," his father replied. "At the same time that work gets along without human life, at that same time it ceases to make human life its final aim; it ceases to value man. Man has never been so unhappy as at this moment when he is accumulating so much. Nowhere is he thought so little of as in the places where this accumulation is going on. That is why the history of the West seems to me to reveal the insufficiency of the guarantee that man offers to man. For man's welfare and happiness we must have the presence and the guarantee of God."

He paused, then added, thoughtfully:

"Perhaps Pascal had caught a glimpse of this. Perhaps his piercing gaze had seen from afar what the methodological myopia of the scholars had not seen."

Suddenly the knight raised his eyes toward the sky, and said:

"But now it is the hour of twilight. Let us pray."

These moments had brought Samba Diallo a renewal of peace. The words of his father had once more restored his serenity, as in former days the words of the teacher had done. There are those who believe and those who do not believe; the division is clear. It leaves no one outside its neatly drawn line.

Thus, there are those who believe. They, as the knight had said, are those who are justified before God. Samba Diallo paused to consider this new step. The idea was just. In effect, he said to himself, the act of faith is an act of allegiance. There is nothing in the believer which does not draw a particular significance from that allegiance. So the action of a believer, if it is voluntary, is different in its essence from the identical material action of a non-believer. So it is with his work. At this moment in his reflections Samba Diallo heard, like an echo brought to him out of his memories, the voice of his teacher, who, many years before, had been commenting on one of the sacred verses of the Word. It is God Who has created us," the teacher was saying, "ourselves and all that we do." And he insisted upon the second part of the sentence, explaining that it flowed, of necessity, from the first. He used to add that the greatness of God was measured by the fact that in spite of such a total legislation man nevertheless felt himself free. "For being in the water, is the fish less free than the bird in the air?" he would say. Now, Samba Diallo had to make an effort to detach his thought from the memory of the teacher.

"If a man is justified of God, the time he takes from prayer to do his work—that is still prayer. . . ." The knight was right. Everything was coherent, satisfying to the mind and spirit. At that moment, so, Samba Diallo had found peace again. The prayer that he offered, there behind the knight, was a prayer in serenity.

When he had finished the prayer, he became lost in his thoughts again. He went over the conclusions the knight had drawn, and set himself to consider them. Always he felt a high degree of pleasure in turning those clear thoughts over in his mind, when he caught up with them, as if to verify their fine quality. Whatever might be the slant at which he took them, he was assured of finding them identical and stable: compelling. This toughness of ideas delighted him. At the same time, he was testing out his intelligence here, as the blade of a razor is tested on the file.

"The work of him who believes is justified of God." That seemed to him true, however he might consider it. To believe: that is to recognize one's own will as a small fragment of the divine will. It follows from this that activity, the creation of will, is the creation of God.

At this moment his thought brought back to him, in memory, another recollection, a page from Descartes. Where had he read that? In the *Méditations Métaphysiques*, perhaps. He no longer remembered. He only recalled the thought of the French master: The rapport between God and man is first of all a rapport of will to will; can there be a rapport more intimate?

"So," he said to himself, "the masters are in agreement. Descartes, as well as the teacher of the Diallobé, as well as my father—they have all experienced the irreducible inflexibility of this idea." Samba Diallo's joy increased with the realization of this convergence.

"What is more," his thought went on, "to proceed from God, will to will, is to recognize His Law, which is a law of justice and harmony among men. Work is not, therefore, a necessary source of conflict between them. . . ."

The darkness had completely fallen by this time. The knight in the dalmatic was still crouched motionless, facing the east. Stretched out on his back beside him, Samba Diallo opened wide unseeing eyes upon the star-studded firmament.

"There is no antagonism between the discipline of faith and the discipline of work. The death of God is not a necessary condition to the survival of man."

Samba Diallo was not seeing the shining firmament, for the same peace reigned in the heavens and in his heart. Samba Diallo was not existing. There were innumerable stars, there was the earth chilled anew by the coming of night, there was the shade, and there was their simultaneous presence.

"It is at the very heart of this presence that thought is born," he reflected, "as on the water a succession of waves is set off around a spot where something has fallen. But there are those who do not believe. . . ."

Samba Diallo suddenly saw the sky. In a flash, he realized its serene beauty.

"There are those who do not believe. . . . We who believe—we cannot abandon our brothers who do not believe. The world belongs to them as much as it does to us. Labor is a law for them as much as it is for us. They are our brothers. Often, their ignorance of God will have come to them as an accident of their labor, in the workyards where our common dwelling is being put up. Can we forsake them?

"In addition, my God, to those who have lost Thee, there are those who, today as since the beginnings of history, have never known Thy grace—can we abandon them? We implore Thee to accept them, as Thou alone knowest how to accept those whom Thou dost accept, for they have built the world with us, whence we are able, with a thought each day less preoccupied, to seek Thee and salute Thee. It must not be at the cost of Thy grace that man conquers his liberty. Must it be so?"

Samba Diallo rose from his place, and opened his mouth to question the knight. But he did not dare.

"What is it?" his father asked.

"I am cold," he said. "I am going to bed."

PART TWO

When Samba Diallo entered the drawing-room, everyone rose with a single movement. Lucienne came to
meet him, rosy and smiling, her hand outstretched.

"Has Socrates at last drunk the hemlock?" she
asked, with a smile in her voice.

Samba Diallo smiled back at her.

"No," he answered. "The sacred vessel has not yet
returned from Delos."

Addressing her parents, Lucienne explained:
"Samba Diallo is preparing a work on the *Phédon* for
our study group, and he is so passionately absorbed in
this task that for a moment I was afraid he was forgetting to come."

Then, turning toward Samba Diallo, she intro-
duced her family: her father, her mother, and her
cousin Pierre, a medical student.

"I hope, Monsieur, that you will excuse us for receiving you like this, in complete simplicity," Madame
Martial said. "Lucienne and I want you to feel entirely
at ease here, as in your own home."

"I thank you for your kindness, Madame, and for
your invitation."

"Then add that you are only making this reply
from politeness," Lucienne's father cried out. "My wife

imagines that your African milieu is distinguished from ours only by a lesser complexity."

Behind the glasses that corrected his vision, the man's face was sparkling with mischief.

Paul Martial was a Protestant pastor. The head that topped a robust, almost massive, body would have seemed prematurely old if it had not been for the freshness of the glance behind those eyeglasses. Beneath a thick and greying thatch of hair gleamed the whiteness of a broad forehead which, in spite of the difference in color, reminded Samba Diallo of the forehead, with its skin hardened by long prostrations, of the teacher of the Diallobé. The long narrow nose overhung a grave, distressful mouth. In the dryness of the lips, their puckering at the moment of speaking, Samba Diallo recognized the unfitness of this mouth for the utterance of futile words. The forehead and eyes, nevertheless, sparkled with serenity, as if to envelop with clarity and reduce to nothingness in light the chaos evoked by the terrific mouth. But at this moment the man was forcing himself to gayety, and seemed entranced by the confusion into which he saw that his remark had plunged his wife.

"You—to put your own thoughts on the lips of others," Madame Martial protested.

"Good thrust, aunt!" said Pierre. Then he turned and addressed himself mainly to Samba Diallo. "You have before you a beautiful embodiment of what you philosophers call, I believe, a dialectic pair. Do you feel a call to arbitrate?"

Monsieur and Madame Martial looked at each other with an air of comic bewilderment.

"My poor Marguerite, you heard?" said Monsieur Martial. "We are a pair of screech-owls. . . ."

They made as if to throw themselves into each other's arms, and everybody burst out laughing. Lucienne, meanwhile, insisted on their sitting down, and went to get the drinks.

When she offered his glass to Samba Diallo he held out his hand to take it, then interrupted the movement halfway.

"Oh, Lucienne, I am truly confused," he said. "I forgot to tell you that I don't drink anything alcoholic. But don't bother to get me anything else. I am not thirsty."

"But yes, of course," Madame Martial put in. "Lucienne, give him a glass of fruit juice. There is some there. No, don't protest!"

Samba Diallo felt crushed. He had lost track of the occasions, since his arrival in France, when the refusal of an offered glass had suddenly and absurdly come close to spoiling the first fragile moments of his contact with other people.

"What, you don't drink? You have never drunk the least drop of alcohol?" demanded Pierre, as if bewildered.

"No," Samba Diallo apologized. "My religion forbids it. I am a Moslem."

"But I have Moslem acquaintances who drink, Arabs, Negroes."

"Yes, I know."

Monsieur Martial looked attentively at Samba Diallo. "How he spoke those words!" he said to himself. "He made his chahâda* wave like a banner in the wind!"

Lucienne and her mother were busying themselves between the kitchen and the dining table. Samba Diallo, who felt the gaze of both Pierre and the pastor fixed upon him, took up his glass of fruit juice and emptied it, to put himself in countenance. He realized that the pastor was addressing him:

"Lucienne has often spoken of you, here at the house. She has been very much impressed by the enthusiasm and the aptitude with which you are carrying on your studies in philosophy."

"Your daughter is too kind, Monsieur. She will have found this flattering way for me to tell you what considerable trouble I am having with those studies."

"Then you intend to teach?"

"Perhaps I shall teach. Everything will depend on what will have happened to me by the time I reach the end of my studies. You know, the fate of us Negro students is a little like that of a courier: at the moment of leaving home we do not know whether we shall ever return."

"And what does that return depend on?" asked Pierre.

"It may be that we shall be captured at the end of our itinerary, vanquished by our adventure itself. It suddenly occurs to us that, all along our road, we have

* Formula of the Moslem profession of faith.

not ceased to metamorphose ourselves, and we see ourselves as other than what we were. Sometimes the metamorphosis is not even finished. We have turned ourselves into hybrids, and there we are left. Then we hide ourselves, filled with shame."

"As for you," said the pastor, with a very sweet smile, "I do not believe that you will ever experience that shame, or that you will lose your way. I believe you are one of those who always return to the sources. Isn't it this attraction of sources, moreover, which has oriented you toward philosophy?"

Samba Diallo hesitated before replying.

"I don't know," he said, at last. "When I think about it now, I can't help wondering if there hasn't also been a little of the morbid attraction of danger. I have chosen the itinerary which is most likely to get me lost."

"Why?" Pierre asked again. "Is it through a will to challenge?"

It was the pastor who answered, addressing Samba Diallo.

"No, I believe it is through honesty. Isn't that so? You have chosen to become acquainted with us through what has appeared to you as most characteristic, most fundamental. But I should like to ask you: from what you have been able to grasp of the history of our thought, has it seemed to you radically foreign, or have you indeed recognized yourself a little, just the same?"

Samba Diallo replied without hesitation, as if he had already pondered this question for a long time.

"It seems to me that this history has undergone an accident which has shifted it and, finally, drawn it away from its plan. Do you understand me? Socrates' scheme of thinking does not seem to me, at bottom, different from that of Saint Augustine, though there was Christ between them. The plan is the same, as far as Pascal. It is still the plan of all the thought which is not occidental."

"What is it?" Pierre asked.

"I do not know. But don't you feel as if the philosophical plan were already no longer the same with Descartes as with Pascal? It is not that they were preoccupied with different problems, but that they occupied themselves with them in different ways. It is not the mystery which has changed, but the questions which are asked of it, and the revelations which are expected from it. Descartes is more niggardly in his quest; if, thanks to this and also to his method, he obtains a greater number of responses, what he reports also concerns us less, and is of little help to us. Don't you think so?"

Pierre's only answer was a dubious pursing of his lips. The pastor smiled.

"Hold firmly to this opinion," he said, "even if it seems to you that you do not back it up sufficiently. It constitutes a line of demarcation, and those who are on your side become fewer every day. What is more, those of the opposition put forth something deceptive by their assurance and their success in piling up partial answers."

Madame Martial came in and called them to the table.

The pastor, who was getting ready to ask a bless-

ing on the meal, noticed that Samba Diallo had preceded him in prayer. The young man had retired
within himself for a brief moment, with an impercept-
ible murmur.

Dinner began. Lucienne turned toward Samba
Diallo:

"You know, Papa just missed starting his ministry
in Africa. He hasn't yet told you about it?"

"Ah?" Samba Diallo's voice had a rising inflection
as he looked at the pastor and his daughter in turn.

"It's an old story, all that." The pastor spoke with
a hint of melancholy. "I dreamed of founding a mission in Africa, in some open countryside where no sol-
dier, no doctor, good or bad, would have preceded
me. We should have presented ourselves supplied only
with the word of God. Our task being one of evangel-
ization, I should carefully have avoided taking anything in, even the least cumbersome and the most use-
ful of medicaments. My wish was that the revelation of
which we should have been the missionaries would owe
nothing except to itself, and for us would be literally
an imitation of Jesus Christ. For the rest, I was not waiting only for the edification of those who would be con-
verted. I was counting, with the help of God, that the
example of your faith would have revived our own,
that the Negro church which we should have raised up
would very quickly have taken over for us in the combat for the faith. . . . When I unbosomed myself of
this project to my superiors, they had no difficulty in
enlightening me as to my naïveté."

When the pastor fell silent, Samba Diallo had the

impression that he had hastened to cut short the evoca-tion of his old dream. "He has not said everything," the young man thought. "He has not told us either that he was not convinced by his superiors, although he sub-mitted to them, or what great debate must have di-vided him from himself."

"I say to myself, for my own part," he said to the pastor, "that it is infinitely regrettable that your dream should not have been followed out."

"Eh? Do you really believe that it was more urgent to send you pastors than to send you physicians?" Lucienne demanded.

"Yes, if you are thus offering me a choice between faith and the health of the body," Samba Diallo replied.

"We must congratulate ourselves that it is only a hypothetical question," Lucienne said. "I am sure that if fate should propose that choice to you—"

"Fate has proposed that choice to me, it is still pro-posing it to me at the present time. My country is dying because it dare not settle this alternative once and for all."

"In my opinion," she retorted, "that is just plain mad."

"Come, come, Lucienne," her mother put in.

The girl's face was pink with both exasperation and confusion. She was turning in succession toward the pastor and Samba Diallo, as if undecided between the two. It seemed that the same feeling moved the two men. In their eyes, on their lips, there was the same look of affectionate disapprobation.

"I did not mean to question the value of faith,"

Lucienne said at last, in a voice that was once more calm. "I only wanted to say that the possession of God ought not to cost man any of his chances."

"I know that very well," Samba Diallo said. "The offensiveness of this choice is something which makes it difficult to admit. Nevertheless it exists—and it seems to me to be a product of your history." Then he added, with, it seemed, an aftermath of asperity, "For my part, if the direction of my country devolved upon me, I should admit your doctors and your engineers only with many reservations, and I do not know whether I should not have combatted them at the first encounter."

"Know at least in what company you would find yourself, in that combat," said Lucienne. "Your cause is defensible, perhaps; the sad thing is that those who defend it do not always have your purity and Papa's. They ally themselves with this cause to cover up designs that would move backward."

Samba Diallo's expression had suddenly grown sad.

2

Having succeeded, with a slow movement, in girding Demba's head with the white turban, the teacher of the Diallobé undertook the interminable task of crouching down on his heels. With his left hand he supported himself on one knee, while the right hand, palm open, was descending, trembling, toward the ground. When it had got so far the left hand followed. Those who were present watched, motionless.

No one in the world, certainly, had crouched down like this so many times in his life as the teacher of the Diallobé, for no one had prayed so much as he. Old age and rheumatism had made of this gesture—still repeated twenty times a day—a grotesque and painful exercise which the watchers, moved and breathless, were following.

The man set himself to bending his knees, so that they might touch the ground. As he did this the whole framework of his body began, with them, to make a cracking sound. Suddenly he collapsed and remained motionless for as long as it took him to get his breath. From one corner of the company around him came a feeble sob, quickly repressed.

The old man, stretched out on the earth on his stomach, rolled over so as to rest on his back, and paused again to breathe. Supporting himself on his bent elbows, he straightened his head and shoulders, and at last reached a sitting position. A sigh rose from those present, which covered the teacher's own smile. Then silence reigned.

"I am nothing," said the teacher, panting. "I beg you to believe with me, like me, that I am nothing: only a minute echo which claimed, while it lasted, to be swollen with the Word. A ridiculous claim. My voice is a thin little sound stifled by what is not my voice. The Word by which my voice claims to be swollen is the universal outflowing. My voice cannot make its miserable sound heard—a sound already twice corked up and imprisoned. The being is there, before it is raised; then it is killed. Do you feel how it is that I am the vain echo?"

"We feel it," said the fool, repressing a new sob.

"The Word weaves together what is, more intimately than the light weaves the day. The Word overflows your destiny, from the side of the project, from the side of the deed, being the three from all eternity. I worship the Word."

"Master, what you say is beyond us," the smith put in.

"I was not speaking to you."

"Speak to us."

The teacher looked at the man, and his gaze seemed to pierce him through and through.

"One morning, then," he said to him, "you wake up. The dark flood has receded far, after a hard upsurge: it is indeed you, and not another in your place, that has awakened. This heavy anxiety that distends your being just as the light spreads—it is you whom it fills; this man who is terrified by being recalled to the thought of death—this is you. You thrust the anxiety aside and get up. You believe in God. You prostrate yourself and pray. This family, devoid of food and certain of eating today—it is your family, waiting for you to feed it. You hate it; you also love it. Here you are smiling at it and brooding over it, as you get up and go out into the street. Those whom you encounter are in your image; you smile at them, they smile at you; you bite them, they bite you; you love them and you loathe them; you approach them, then you move away from them. You get the best of them and they hit you. You return to your home, exhausted and weighed down with food. Your family eats, you smile, they smile, satisfied; you are annoyed: you must go out again. This family, in need of nourishment and sure of eating, it is your family waiting for you to feed it. This man who rebels against being recalled to the thought of his death, it is you—who thrusts that thought aside and gets up. You believe in God, you prostrate yourself and pray. . . . Of whom have I spoken?"

"Of me, master," said the smith, cast down.

"No," said the teacher, "it was of myself."

For the second time, the fool burst into sobs, shameless and powerful.

"Was anyone ever so familiar with the summits as this old man who weeps over his failure to reach them?" Demba was thinking. "He suffers from giddiness, and he gives place to me. He believes that his giddiness is due to his great age. He is right. My youth will allow of more temerity. It is more obtuse, and it is well that it should be so. He hesitates, I will make short work of problems. But is this indeed a matter of age? Samba Diallo, at my age, would also have hesitated; that is certain. Then, I am obtuse. But I shall make short work of problems."

The Most Royal Lady expressed her satisfaction:

"It is well that this young man should replace the teacher. He has not, he never will have, that preference of the old man for traditional values, even those that are condemned and moribund, over the triumphant values that are assailing us. This young man is bold. He is not paralysed by the sense of what is sacred. He has no feeling for background. He will know better than anyone else how to welcome the new world. As for my young cousin—Samba Diallo also will have lived his life, spiritually. Poor child, he should have been born as the contemporary of his ancestors. I believe that he would have been the spiritual guide for them. Today—today—"

"Why did it happen that I let him go?" the chief of the Diallobé asked himself. "He is of the same age as this young man who has just been made teacher of the Diallobé. I would have made him chief of the Diallobé in my place, unless the teacher had chosen him to wear his turban. He would have kept the movement of the Diallobé within the confines of the narrow track that winds between their past and those new fields where they want to pasture and gambol and be lost. Instead, here am I today, faced by this young man, alone with him, abandoned by my old companion and master."

The old companion, meanwhile, was laughing. The chief of the Diallobé gazed at him, curious as to what new shift of mood was amusing him, when the tears he had drawn from the fool were scarcely dried. It was precisely the fool who was now moving him to delight. Buttoned up in his military tunic, the madman had knelt down opposite the teacher, very near, and was speaking to him, holding his arm the while. The same laughter relaxed both their faces, very close to each other, as if they were seeking not to be overheard by any of the people around them.

"Will you say the prayer now, master?" the chief asked.

The old man gently pushed the fool away, faced Demba, and held out his arms in a gesture of prayer. All those present followed his example.

At the end of the prayer Demba announced that beginning the next day he would change the schedules at the Hearth. In this way, all the parents who might so desire would be able to send their sons to the foreign school. "For," he concluded, "the Prophet—may benediction be upon him!—has said, 'You are to go in search of Knowledge, even if it must be as far as China.' "

At first glance, Samba Diallo recognized the writing of the chief of the Diallobé. He seized the letter and went running up the stairs.

His cousin had written:

"How can man, whose fate it is to grow old and then to die—how can he claim to govern: which is the art of having, at every moment, the age and the desires of the generation which changes and does not grow old? No one has known the country of the Diallobé as I have known it. I was the eminence which welcomed and reflected the first rays that came from the depths of the world. Always, I went ahead, and I felt neither anxiety nor self-conceit. But at the same time I was the rear-guard. I had never been satisfied that the desires of the last of the Diallobé should not have been fulfilled. Those were good times, when I controlled this country without any one of us stealing a march on any other."

Samba Diallo paused for a moment in his reading. "He was himself, he was the country," he thought, "and this unity was not broken by any division. Oh, my country, within the circle of your frontiers the one and the many were still linked together yesterday. I know very well that I did not dream that! The chief and the multitude, power and obedience, they were of the same breed, and cousins close-born. Knowledge and faith flowed from a common source and fed the same sea. Within your frontiers it was still given to man to enter the world by the great portal. I have been the sovereign who, one step away from the master, could cross the threshold of all unity, penetrate to the intimate heart of being, invade it and make one with it, without any one of us overstepping the other. Chief of the Diallobé, why have I had to cross the frontier of your kingdom?"

The chief's letter went on:

"Today everything fled and crumbled around my immobility, as the sea does along a reef. I am no longer the point of reference, the landmark; I am the obstacle which men walk around in order not to hit it. If you could see their expressions as they watch me! They are full of solicitude and pity—of brutal determination also. The hour strikes when, if I had this choice at my disposal, I should choose to die.

"Alas, I cannot even do as your old teacher did, lay aside that part of myself which belongs to men and leave it within their hands, while I withdraw.

"One evening he came to me, according to that old custom which you know. The fool, who never leaves him now, was holding him by the arm, and they were both laughing like children, pleased to be together. 'Here is the valley about to take leave of the mountain,' the fool said, and I suddenly felt sad through and through, as I had not done since the death of my father. 'The deep valley where the heart of the world is beating,' the fool went on. But the teacher interrupted him: 'Hush! Be still! You have promised me to behave yourself. If you do not, we will go away again.' At that the fool fell silent.

"I did not take my eyes off the teacher. He was not sad.

" 'Tomorrow,' he said to me, 'I shall put the turban on Demba, if it please God.'

" 'That can only result in good, if you have so decided,' I acquiesced.

" 'Have you perceived how stupid I am?' he inquired. 'For a long time I have felt that I was the only obstacle to this country's happiness. I have pretended not to be that obstacle. I was hoping—but it is only now that I know this—that the country would carry me over, so that it might obtain its happiness without my losing my good conscience.'

" 'You are not fair to yourself,' I said to him.

" 'What do you know about it?' he retorted.

" 'It is not you yourself whom you should defend, but God.'

" 'What has He just been doing here? You see, it is yourself that I have been taking advantage of. God was my great treasure-trove. I suggested, by my attitude, that it was He whom I was defending. But, I ask you, can God be defended from man? Who can do that? Who has that right? To whom does God belong? Who has not the right to love Him or to scoff at Him? Think it over, chief of the Diallobé: the freedom to love God or hate Him is God's ultimate gift, which no one can take from man.'

" 'Master,' I said to him, 'I am speaking of those men who live in the country of the Diallobé. In our eyes they are like children. We have the duty of taking their liberty from them, in order to use it to their advantage.'

" 'You,' he responded, 'of you, nothing could be more true. But not of me.'

"Then he was silent for a long time. When he spoke again, it was with an aftermath of sadness:

" 'I have thought this infamous thing: that God could be an obstacle to the happiness of men. How stupid that is, my God, how stupid I have been! The truth is, Oh, God, that there are always cunning men to make use of Thee. Offering Thee and refusing Thee, as if Thou hast belonged to them, with the aim of keeping other men in obedience to them! Chief of the Diallobé, reflect that the revolt of the multitude against these shysters may take on the significance of a revolt against God—when on the contrary it is the most holy of all the holy wars!'

"He talked to me in this vein for a long time, brushing away all my objections, weeping over his own base deeds. The fool, in his corner, had gone to sleep."

Samba Diallo let the letter fall from his hand.

"No!" he thought. "What have their problems to do with me? I have the right to do as this old man has done: to withdraw from the arena of their confused desires, their weaknesses, their flesh, to retire within myself. After all, I am only myself. I have only me."

He got up, undressed himself, and prepared for bed. Late in the night he realized that he had forgotten to make his evening prayer, and he had to disturb his rest to get up again and pray.

"My God, dost Thou not then remember me? I am that soul whom Thou hast made to weep in filling him with Thy grace. I beg Thee, do not allow me to become the utensil which I feel to be emptying itself already. I have not asked Thee to bring to flower that glow which, one day, perceived that it was burning. Thou hast wanted me. Thou wouldst not know how to forget me like that. I would not agree, alone with us two, to suffer from Thy absence. . . .

"Remember, Lord, how Thou hast nourished my existence from Thine. So time is nourished by duration. I felt Thee to be the deep sea from which spreads out my thought and, at the same time, everything. Through Thee, I was the same wave as the whole.

"They say that the human being is quartered from nothingness, is an archipelago of which the islands do not remain underneath, drowned as they are by nothingness. They say that the sea, which is such that everything not itself floats there, is nothingness. They say that the truth is nothingness, and being, a multiple avatar.

"And Thou, Thou blessest their erring ways. Thou attachest success to man as one side of anything is attached to its reverse side. Under the flood of their spreading delusion fortune crystallizes its gems. Thy Truth no longer weighs very heavily upon us, my God. . . ."

Morning found Samba Diallo crouched, wide awake, on the prayer rug, his limbs stiff with pain.

He thought, "I must write to my father."

3

June was drawing to a close, and already the heat in Paris was oppressive.

Samba Diallo was walking slowly down the Boulevard Saint-Michel. Benumbed by the heat, he was walking half-asleep. A firm-spun thread of clear thought was filtering with some difficulty through the heavy down of his sensations, as a current of cool water courses through the inert mass of a tepid sea. Samba Diallo was forcing himself to concentrate what remained of his attention on the point where that slight gleam of thought came through.

"These streets are bare," he was noticing. "No, they are not empty. One meets objects of flesh in them, as well as objects of metal. Apart from that, they are empty. Ah! One also encounters events. Their succession congests time, as the objects congest the street. Time is obstructed by their mechanical jumble. One does not perceive the background of time, and its slow current. I walk. One foot before, one foot behind, one foot before, one foot behind: one-two, one-two. No! I must not think: one-two, one-two. I must think of something else. One-two, one-two. . . . Malte Laurids Brigge. . . . Look! Yes—I am Malte Laurids Brigge. Like him, I am walking down the Boulevard Saint-Michel. There is nothing, nothing but me, nothing but

my body, I mean to say. I touch it. Through the pocket
of my trousers I touch my thigh. I think of my right big
toe. There is nothing but my right big toe. Otherwise,
their street is empty, their time is encumbered, their
soul is silted up down there, under my right big toe, and
under the events and under the objects of flesh and the
objects of metal—the objects of flesh and—"

Suddenly he was conscious of an obstacle, there
in front of his body. He tried to turn aside. The obstacle was stubborn. Samba Diallo knew that his attention was being solicited.

"How do you do, Monsieur?" said the obstacle.

It was as if this voice were waking him. In front of
Samba Diallo an old Negro was standing. In spite of his
advanced age, which had not bent his body, he must
have stood at the same height as the young man. He
was wearing old clothes, and the collar of his shirt was
of doubtful cleanliness. A black beret cut across his
thatch of white hair, and its edges had thus the sem-
blance of being buried in a skull-cap. He was carrying
a white cane, and Samba Diallo fixed his attention on
his eyes, to see if he was blind. No, the man was not
blind, though the whole central surface of his left eye
was covered by a white film. His right eye showed no
abnormality, though it presented the stigmata of fatigue. As he smiled, his mouth disclosed old yellow
teeth, far apart and out of line.

"How do you do, Monsieur?" Samba Diallo responded in his turn. He was wide awake now, and had
a sense of great well-being.

"Excuse an old man for stopping you unceremoniously, like this. But we are compatriots, are we not? What country, then, do you come from?"

"From the country of the Diallobé."

"Ah, Black Africa! I have known your people well, commencing with your first two Deputies, Blaise Diagne and Galandou Diouf, who were both Senegalese, I believe. But what would you think of our taking a table somewhere—that is, if you are not in a hurry?"

They settled themselves on the terrace of a café.

"My name is Pierre-Louis," the old man said. "I have been a magistrate, and I have served to some extent in all parts of your country, over a period of twenty years. After that, at the appointed time, I retired. I was beginning to get sick and tired of the drawbacks of the bloody system. Then I stepped down from the bench to go to the other side of the bar. For twelve years I defended my compatriots, from Gabon and Cameroon, against the State and the French settlers. They're a bad lot, those bloody settlers."

"Where are you from, exactly?" Samba Diallo inquired.

"I do not know. My great-grandfather was called Mohammed Kati—yes, Kati, like the author of the *Tarikh El Fettâch*—and he was from the same region as his great namesake, the very heart of the old empire of the Mali. My great-grandfather was made a slave, and sent to the Islands, where he was rebaptised Pierre-Louis Kati. He dropped the name of Kati so as not to dishonor it, and called himself simply Pierre-Louis. What will you have to drink?" he asked Samba Diallo.

When the waiter had gone to fill their orders, Pierre-Louis turned back to Samba Diallo.

"What was I saying? Ah, yes, I was telling you that the settlers and the French State were living then off the poor folk of Cameroon and Gabon. Ha, ha, ha!"

The man laughed as if he were coughing, from the depths of his chest, with his mouth open, and without the least participation from his face—either his lips or his eyes—in this hilarity. The laughter did not increase, and, without any diminution, it stopped as suddenly as it had begun.

"In Cameroon, all the litigations came from the French claim that they had inherited more rights than their German predecessors had actually possessed. Have you studied law, Monsieur?"

"No."

"That is too bad. All the Blacks ought to study the law of the Whites—French, English, Spanish, the law of all the colonizing peoples, as well as their languages. You must have studied the French language—I mean to say, you must have made a profound study of it. What are you specializing in?"

"I am finishing work for a degree in philosophy."

"Ah, excellent, my son. That is very good. For, you know, they are there, completely, in their law and their language. Their law, their language, constitute the very texture of their genius, in what is greatest in it and also what is most pernicious. Let us see, what was I saying? Oh, yes. . . . Then, the French, holding a mandate from the League of Nations, could not have been in possession of greater rights than the men who gave them the mandate. Now the League of Nations itself—do you know what it inherited from Germany, in the matter of Cameroon? It inherited a lawsuit! No more! Ha, ha, ha! I amaze you, eh? I have the documents at home. I will show them to you. You will see there that the Germans had signed treaties of friendship and the establishment of a protectorate with the sovereigns of Cameroon. The Kaiser negotiated with the aforesaid sovereigns on terms of equality, and that is how it was that the princes of Cameroon were educated in the imperial court itself, with the sons of the German Empire.

"People have wanted us to believe," the old man went on, "that the Germans were racists—fundamentally, more than the other white nations of the West. That is false. Hitler, yes, and his Nazis, as well as all the world's Fascists, without doubt; but otherwise the Germans are no more racist than the civil or military settlers of all nationalities. Remember Kitchener at Khartoum, the French armies in the conquest of Algeria, Cortez in Mexico, and so on. What is true is that the Germans are metaphysicians. To convince them there must be arguments of pure transcendence, and their racists have understood that. Elsewhere, men are jurists, and they justify themselves by the Code. Elsewhere, again, they fight for God, and they justify themselves before Him in their purpose of straightening out His twisted creatures—or massacring them if they resist. . . . What was I saying? Oh, yes. . . . Then, all went well between the Germans and Cameroon, insofar as the treaties were observed. With the agreement of the princes, the Germans encouraged the cultivation of the export trade, in buying the Negroes' products at a high price, and in kicking their behinds, without any racism, believe me, if they were not willing to work. The scuffle began when the Germans, under the pretext of I do not know what necessity for cleaning up the country, claimed the right to pillage the lands of the Cameroon people. The princes appointed a lawyer, in Germany itself, to defend their cause. German justice decided in favor of the Cameroons, and the German State left the matter in abeyance because of the outbreak of war. The French replaced the Germans in Cameroon. I ask you, could they claim to have inherited more than a lawsuit?"

"If that is the case, obviously—" Samba Diallo began, but Pierre-Louis interrupted him:

"That is the case, Monsieur. I, in my turn, had the honor of taking over the assignment to defend the natural rights of the people of Cameroon over their land. I went as far as Geneva to acquit myself of this task. It is a lion that you have before you, Monsieur, a lion that roars and leaps forward every time a blow is struck at the sacred cause of liberty!"

In his frenzy the old man was indeed tossing a lion's mane over the coffee cups. Within Samba Diallo a strong feeling of sympathy for the old Negro was rising like a warm wave.

"This very day," the young man was thinking, as Pierre-Louis prattled on, "in these streets where I felt, in despair, that time was covered over by the ignoble sediment of event and object, here is the soul of the times, here is the passion of revolution, as well as its mad dreams, surging up before me. Beneath the mane of this old black lion there is the same breath which stirred Saint-Just, which continues to stir our kind. But in truth, from Saint-Just to this old lunatic Pierre-Louis, the succession has grown heavy, like ripening fruit. The French Revolution is the adolescence of revolution, so it is better embodied in an adolescent than in anyone else. Is it the great evening of revolution which is announced with the twentieth century? See how feverishly it barricades itself in the shade, behind the black skin of the last of the slaves, Pierre-Louis! Is that in order to wage his last fight?"

"You have not told me your name, Monsieur," the old man said.

Samba Diallo gave a start as he answered:

"I am called Samba Diallo. I believe I have already told you that I am a student. Here is my address," and he handed Pierre-Louis a card.

"Here is mine," the latter responded. "I should like to have you at my house, one of these days. I will not bore you too much. Besides, my little family will look out for that, you shall see."

They rose, and Pierre-Louis took leave of his new friend.

4

As soon as he entered the café Samba Diallo caught sight of Lucienne's raised hand, signalling to him. He made his way toward her and held out his own hand, smiling.

" 'The bird is not on the flower, balanced by the wind,

And the flower has no scent, and the bird does not sigh,

Except better to enchant the air breathed forth by your bosom.' "

With this declamation he sat down.

She withdrew her hand and made a gesture for him to shut his mouth.

"Idiot!" she said.

He dropped his head, pulled down the corners of his mouth, sniffled, and gave such a good imitation of a child in great chagrin that she burst out laughing.

"If I did not know you as such an old Turk I should have sworn that you had been drinking," the girl said, with the gravity of a doctor announcing a diagnosis.

"But, see, I have not yet had anything to drink. However, I am about to have something."

He signalled to the waiter and ordered coffee. Then he turned toward Lucienne.

"Coffee does me no good, I know, but I do not stop

drinking it. It is by this sign, along with others, that I recognize the presence of Fatality among us. . . ."

Lucienne, her elbows on the table, her chin in her open hands, was now fixing upon him a gaze which expressed resignation.

"Good," he said, "here is my coffee. I shall say nothing more. I am listening to you."

The waiter set down the coffee and Samba Diallo began to drink it, while he watched Lucienne.

He had dreaded this meeting a little. Since the evening when he had dined at the girl's house they had seen each other very little, principally on the occasion of the examinations at the end of the year's work. There was, to be sure, an excuse which Samba Diallo could plead for that: the inspections. But Lucienne knew how he made use of his time, and she knew that the approach of the examinations had changed that program very little. She knew that, whatever the circumstances, if he had wanted to see her he would have found the necessary time. He felt that she had not been deceived.

But no more could he avow the reason for his sudden withdrawal: the impossibility of enduring any longer the calm inquiry of those blue eyes which the girl had fixed on him since the first moments of their meeting. What did Lucienne want?

One day, after the examinations in which they had both been successful, he had received a note from her:

"If the distinction with which you passed the examinations has not turned your head, perhaps you will remember me?" Then the letter continued:

"You see, I am forcing myself to joke. Unfortunately, I have every reason to believe that the reason I have not seen you is, rather, my stupid attitude when you came to dinner at the house. I had merely believed that with a philosopher I could argue in complete freedom, without fear of bringing old susceptibilities out of ambush. I should like to explain myself about all that, if you are available. Make an appointment for me."

He had fixed this rendezvous and had come to it not without apprehension, afraid of all that she might divine in him. He had hoped to maintain the conversation on the playful level they had adopted, but it seemed that Lucienne, for her part, had no such intention this time.

"I have never seen you in such an amiable mood," she stated, with a smile.

"I was working on you. I have other talents, and if you wish—"

She grasped his hand.

"Samba Diallo, did I really vex you, in speaking as I did, the other evening?"

"Certainly not! Besides, I don't see what could have vexed me."

"I don't know. Afterward, I thought that I had been a little quick-tempered. In any case, I didn't want to offend you."

She hesitated, as if she were seeking to add something more, in order to win forgiveness from her companion.

"Lucienne, Lucienne, you do not know how to arrange your effects. There, by all the evidence, we must go back to Shakespeare: 'If, in shooting my arrow over the roof,' and so on. See *Hamlet*."

"Are you going to listen until I have finished?" she demanded, stamping her foot.

He became serious again.

"Yes, Lucienne, I am listening."

"Here, then. . . . I want to tell you also that I am a member of the Communist Party."

"I knew that."

"You knew it?"

"Yes, I have seen you distributing leaflets."

One day, in fact, he had caught sight of her distributing some leaflets at the door of the Sorbonne. He had hastened his steps, taken a leaflet from the hand of another girl who was also distributing them, and had gone quickly away, for fear of Lucienne's seeing him. At the corner of the street he had opened up the paper. It was signed by the Communist Party. At the same instant, an infinity of little actions he had observed, words he had noted, had converged in his memory and had ended by convincing him. He realized, nevertheless, that this discovery was not surprising him very much, as if since their meeting he had thought that this girl could be moved only by loyalties of this order. He had felt a new upswelling of esteem for her. He wondered that a Protestant minister's own daughter, child of M. Martial's wide-sweeping intelligence, should have lived through the aridity of this Damascus road in reverse. What Samba Diallo knew of Lucienne's intelligence and culture convinced him that this spiritual adventure had not been banal on the one hand or something to be conjured away on the other, but that it had indeed been arduous, lived through in clarity from beginning to end. It did not seem to Samba Diallo that he would have had the sweep of mind to go through such an adventure.

". . . And you see," he added slowly, "I have conceived a new upsurge of admiration for you."

She blushed a little.

"I accept your admiration, and I shall wear it as an ornament henceforth," she said. "But, it only enriches me. . . ."

She hesitated, lowered her eyes.

Her hands on the table were folding and unfolding the paper bill of fare left there by the waiter. Her cheeks were pink; but by the obstinacy of her little forehead, the regularity of her breathing, one guessed that she was determined to follow through her thought to the end.

It was Samba Diallo, however, who spoke. A light had suddenly come on in his mind. He understood what his fair-haired companion wanted of him. From then on, he took the offensive.

"Lucienne, my combat goes beyond yours in every sense."

He had leaned down over the table, and thus he was taking on the appearance of some strange and enormous bird of prey, with wings spread. He seemed suddenly to be filled with profound exaltation.

"You have not only raised yourself above Nature. You have even turned the sword of your thought against her: you are fighting for her subjection—that is your combat, isn't it? As for me, I have not yet cut the umbilical cord which makes me one with her. The supreme dignity to which, still today, I aspire is to be the most sensitive and the most filial part of her. Being Nature herself, I do not dare to fight against her. I never open up the bosom of the earth, in search of my food, without demanding pardon, trembling, beforehand. I never strike a tree, coveting its body, without making fraternal supplication to it. I am only that end of being where thought comes to flower."

Lucienne's big blue eyes were fixed, in all their wide extent, upon Samba Diallo. Around those eyes her face was no more than a vague aureole of white and pink.

"In that way, my thought goes far behind yours, back into the penumbra of our origins," he said.

Samba Diallo had relaxed in his chair. He seemed now to be speaking to himself, with deep melancholy.

Lucienne seized and pressed his hand, which was lying on the table. He gave a little shiver.

"But no, I am not afraid," he protested, as if he wished to forestall words of compassion. "No, you see it is my good fortune that now you are standing there: I shall catch sight of your blonde head, and I shall know that I am not alone."

He suddenly withdrew his hand, and leaned down over the table once more.

"Let us hide nothing, meanwhile. By your own avowal, you will consider your task completed when you have freed the last proletarian from his poverty and invested him with dignity again. You even say that your tools of action, become useless, will wither away, so that nothing stands between the naked body of man and liberty. As for me, I do not fight for liberty, but for God."

Lucienne had to keep herself from bursting into laughter. He saw her smile nevertheless, and, paradoxically, smiled himself, relaxing still further. There was the same defiance in their two smiles.

"I should like to ask you an indiscreet question," she said. "Don't answer if it embarrasses you."

He smiled again.

"I have no choice. Not to answer would be a confession. I shall answer, then."

"If someone proposed to you—if a psychiatrist, for instance, proposed curing your people of that part of themselves which weighs them down, would you accept?"

"Ah, because you think that that would be a matter for psychoanalysis? And, first of all, I am surprised at this appeal to psychoanalysis from a Marxist."

"I didn't say that. I said a doctor, as I would have said a priest or no matter who. Would you accept deliverance?"

"That does not seem to me possible."

"In passing, I admire your impeccable defense. But please answer my question."

Samba Diallo hesitated, and seemed embarrassed.

"I don't know," he said at last.

"Very well, that's enough for me," and Lucienne's face brightened. "I know now that your heart is possessed by your being a Negro—your Negroness, if I may coin a word."

"I confess that I do not like the word, and I don't always understand what it would be meant to cover."

"That you don't like the word is proof of your good taste," said Lucienne, simply.

She settled herself back on the banquette, leaned her head to one side, and smiled slightly.

"You have delved deeply into the Russian mind of the nineteenth century," she said, "the Russian writers, poets, artists. I know that you love that century. It was filled with the same disquiet, the same impassioned and ambiguous torment. To be the extreme eastern end of Europe? Not to be the western bridgehead of Asia? The intellectuals could neither answer these questions nor avoid them. As you with the word I coined, so they did not like to hear talk of 'Slavism.' Yet who among them has not bent the knee, in filial devotion, before Holy Russia?"

Samba Diallo interrupted:

"I was saying just that to you! And no priest or doctor would be able to do anything for this torment."

"Yes, but Lenin?"

Samba Diallo straightened himself in his chair and looked closely at Lucienne. The girl had continued to sit calmly in her place. She had simply ceased to smile, and was regarding Samba Diallo with, it seemed, a slight anxiety.

"Samba Diallo," she said, "the milk that has nourished you, from the breast of the country of the Diallobé, is very sweet and very noble. Be indignant whenever anyone contests that, and correct the cretin who would doubt you because you are a Negro. But know also that the more tender the mother is, and the sooner comes the moment for thrusting her aside—"

Samba Diallo looked straight into Lucienne's eyes and, with a beating heart, said, slowly but distinctly, "I believe that I prefer God to my mother."

In the middle of the stream, Samba Diallo suddenly stopped rowing and leaned back comfortably in his seat. Opposite him, at the other end of the boat, Lucienne, with her face lifted toward the sun, seemed to be asleep.

He took a long breath, stretched himself, looked at the sky, and smiled.

"I should have wished that the heat of the sun would suddenly abate, that the sky would become a little more blue, that the water of the river would flow more swiftly and make more sound. The universe ought to scintillate all around us. Lucienne, is that not possible? When I was a child I was master of that. I achieved new mornings whenever I wanted them. And you?"

She had opened her eyes and was looking at him, without moving nevertheless.

"Never," she said, "except when I went to the country; and even there I just barely got mornings—'ameliorated,' but never those that you evoked."

A long silence followed.

"Tell me, Lucienne—don't laugh at me today—even if I seem to you ridiculous, don't laugh. On this day I should like to plunge, plunge into myself, to the farthest depths of myself, shamelessly. I should so much like to know whether I have only dreamed that happiness I remember, or whether it existed."

"I won't laugh. What happiness?"

"The scene is the same. It has to do with the same house, hemmed in by a sky more or less blue, a countryside more or less animated, water running, trees growing, men and animals living there. The scene is the same, I still recognize it."

She sat up straight and rested her elbow on the edge of the boat.

"What happiness?" she asked again.

"Lucienne, that scene, it is a sham! Behind it, there is something a thousand times more beautiful, a thousand times more true! But I can no longer find that world's pathway."

5

Samba Diallo pressed the button of the bell and waited.
Behind the door he was conscious of the abrupt silence
of voices that had been animated. The door opened.

"Come in, Monsieur."

Before him stood a young girl, smiling. So fascinated was he by this apparition that in spite of being
invited to enter Samba Diallo did not stir. She was tall,
and well got up, so to speak, in a close-fitting jersey
whose black color heightened the warm sunset tint of
her throat, her face, and her arms. A heavy mass of
black hair made an aureole around her head and flowed
weightily down to her shoulders, where it mingled
with, no more than it was distinguished from, the con-
spicuous black of the jersey. Her neck was slender without being thin, and its slimness emphasized the solidity
of a firm throat. On the sunset glow of her face shone
the black onyx of enormous eyes, their reflection alter-
nately held back and offered forth in a timid smile.

"Come in, Monsieur," she repeated. "We have been
expecting you."

Samba Diallo stammered, in confusion: "Excuse
me."

He went in and waited while the girl closed the
door behind him. Then he followed her, and his glance
lingered on the slow undulation of head and shoulders

that animated the rhythm of legs which were long and which he guessed to be delicately built, in their prolongation of small feet shod in moccasins.

At the door of the drawing-room, Samba Diallo was welcomed by a burst of laughter that he knew well.

"Ha, ha, ha! Here he is! Here is the new man. He is young, he is new, he—"

"Pierre-Louis, introduce us to this gentleman, and stop chattering like an old fool."

The woman who had just spoken was a fat half-breed, covered with jewels, who was fixing a maternal gaze upon Samba Diallo.

"Good, good," the old fool complied with his orders. "Young man, this is my wife, Adèle. Such as you see her, in spite of her shrieks, she is of royal blood, being a Gabonaise princess."

So speaking, Pierre-Louis was keeping at a prudent distance from the fat princess. Samba Diallo bowed and took the heavy hand, abundantly adorned with rings, which was held out to him.

"That ray of sun down there, which is trying to hide from your gaze, that is my granddaughter. She has only one single imperfection, which, I must add, is not apparent at first glance: she is called Adèle, also."

Samba Diallo was grateful to the beringed princess for the projectile—a folding fan—which she was waving back and forth over Pierre-Louis' head. The laughter and movement around the room screened his confusion at the moment when he bowed before the apparition of the doorway and clasped a little hand which he thought he felt trembling in his.

"And here are my two sons, Captain Hubert Pierre-Louis, who is Adèle's father, and Marc, who is an engineer."

Samba Diallo exchanged two rugged handclasps.

"That," concluded Pierre-Louis, comically, "will be all for this evening."

"You have greatly impressed our father, Samba Diallo," said Marc. "He has done nothing but talk of you."

Samba Diallo showed his surprise, and was about to protest, when the beringed princess relieved him.

"I know the reason for Pierre-Louis' enthusiasm," she said. "You listened to him. Nothing impresses him so much—and, for the rest, myself also. I have known from that what an education you have."

Everybody laughed, and Samba Diallo profited by that to yield to a furious desire to look at Adèle.

The girl, seated on the rug with her head against Pierre-Louis' knee, was fixing her great eyes on Samba Diallo.

The young man, seeing that, had a sense of pleasure which he immediately regretted; then the regret itself surprised him.

"Come, come," he said to himself. "One would say that Mbara was stirring. Look at him sending vulgar winks toward a young girl whom he is seeing for the first time." Mbara, the typical name for a slave in the country of the Diallobé, was the soubriquet that Samba Diallo's parents would use, when he was a child, to make him ashamed of some bad behavior.

He answered Marc:

"It is I who am grateful to your father for having conjured away the discouragement which was slowly pervading me, when I met him a month ago. I don't know whether you have at times had that poignant impression of vacuity which the streets of this city may give—streets nevertheless so noisy in other respects. There is, as it were, a great absence, one does not know of what. I was the victim of this sensation when I encountered your father, and I have had the feeling that he set me afloat in the current again."

"You live alone?" Hubert inquired, practically.

"No, it is not that," Marc interposed. "I have often heard colored men speak as Samba Diallo is speaking. I believe, for my part, that this impression comes from the fact that, paradoxically, they expect to find in Paris what they have left behind in order to come here. Isn't that your opinion, Samba Diallo?"

"I don't think it is the material environment of my country that I miss, if that is what you mean to say."

"Ah." Marc was interested, and spoke on a note of inquiry. "Then try to explain. You know, my father sent me here when I was a very young child, but I also feel a stranger in this country. I should very much like to know—"

He did not finish the sentence, and waited. Samba Diallo hesitated, not knowing what to say. His eyes sought those of Pierre-Louis, but the old man seemed to be waiting also.

"It is difficult," Samba Diallo began at last. "It might be said that I see less fully here than in the country of the Diallobé. I no longer feel anything directly.

You know, on reflection all this seems ridiculous to me. It may be, after all, that what I regret is not my country so much as my childhood."

"Go on trying. Tell us the form that your nostalgia takes."

"It seems to me, for example, that in the country of the Diallobé man is closer to death. He lives on more familiar terms with it. His existence acquires from it something like an aftermath of authenticity. Down there, there existed between death and myself an intimacy, made up at the same time of my terror and my expectation. Whereas here death has become a stranger to me. Everything combats it, drives it back from men's bodies and minds. I forget about it. When I search for it in my thought, I see only a dried-up sentiment, an abstract eventuality, scarcely more disagreeable for me than for my insurance company."

"In sum," said Marc, laughing, "you are complaining of no longer living your death."

They all laughed, and Samba Diallo, wholly acquiescent, laughed with them. Then he went on, seriously:

"It still seems to me that in coming here I have lost a privileged mode of acquaintance. In former times the world was like my father's dwelling: everything took me into the very essence of itself, as if nothing could exist except through me. The world was not silent and neuter. It was alive. It was aggressive. It spread out. No scholar ever had such knowledge of anything as I had, then, of being."

After a short silence he added:

"Here, now, the world is silent, and there is no longer any resonance from myself. I am like a broken balafong, like a musical instrument that has gone dead. I have the impression that nothing touches me any more."

Pierre-Louis' laughter resounded, short and harsh, through the room.

"Ha, ha, ha! I know what it is. It is not the material absence of your native soil that keeps you in a state of suspended animation, it is its spiritual absence. The West passes you by, you are ignored, you are useless—and that at a time when you yourself can no longer pass by the West. Then you succumb to the complex of the Unloved. You feel that your position is precarious."

Samba Diallo looked at Pierre-Louis, and this time it was not Adèle's eyes that held him. The old fellow was grave, almost sad. "I know now the reason for this old man's madness," Samba Diallo said to himself. "He has been too clear-headed through the course of a too-long life."

"It is only the intellectuals who suffer from that," Captain Hubert cut in. "From the moment that the West agrees to give, what does it matter if it refuses to take? For my part, I am not embarrassed by that."

"No," Samba Diallo objected. "On the contrary, Captain, it is this attitude of yours which seems impossible to me, other than in theory. I am not a distinct country of the Diallobé facing a distinct Occident, and appreciating with a cool head what I must take from it and what I must leave with it by way of counterbalance. I have become the two. There is not a clear mind deciding between the two factors of a choice. There is a strange nature, in distress over not being two."

But Marc was addressing Pierre-Louis:

"I should have liked to find an argument to refute what you have just said. For it seems to me that in a sense you have condemned us. How would the West have been able to pass us by if our message had not been, in some fashion, superfluous? The West victoriously pursues its investiture of the actual. There is no break in its advance. There is no instant that is not filled with this victory. It is not to the leisure to philosophize, of which we are making use at the present time, that we owe the efficacious vigor of the effort by which the world is maintained over our heads like a shelter in the tempest. Can anything exist outside that effort, in consequence, which would have a meaning? I see very well what distinguishes us from them. Our first move is not to conquer, as they do, but to love. We also have our vigor, which takes us at once straight to the intimate heart of a thing. Our knowledge of it is so intense that its fullness intoxicates us. Then we have a sensation of victory. But where is that victory? The object is intact, the man is not stronger."

Samba Diallo became excited.

"As for me," he said, "I saw in your father's words another reach of thought—how shall I say it?—more historic. The consequence of it would be less hopeless. It is not in a difference of nature between the West and what is not the West that I should see the explanation of the opposition in their destinies. If there were a difference of nature, it would follow in effect that if the

West is right, and speaks in a loud voice, what is not the West is necessarily wrong and ought to be silent; that if the West moves beyond its borders and colonizes, this situation is in the nature of things and is definitive. . . ."

"Sure enough!" cried Pierre-Louis.

Samba Diallo began to smile then, suddenly assailed by a memory.

"I have an elderly cousin," he said, "in whose mind reality never loses its just claims. She has not yet emerged from the astonishment into which the defeat and colonization of the Diallobé plunged her. They call her the Most Royal Lady. I should have not gone to the foreign school, and I should not be here this evening, if it had not been for her desire to find an explanation for our defeat. The day I went to take leave of her she said to me again, 'Go find out, among them, how one can conquer without being in the right.'"

"There is a woman who would not let herself tell tales about it, at least. She must be a very great princess. . . ."

As he said this, Pierre-Louis sent a sidelong glance toward the beringed princess, who had lost interest in the talk and, with Adèle, was going back and forth between the kitchen and the dining-table.

"Then you were saying?" Marc put in, addressing himself to Samba Diallo.

The latter seemed, then, to be in a hurry.

"I don't think that this difference exists in nature," he said again, "I believe that it is artificial, accidental. Only, the artifice has grown stronger with time, covering up what is of nature. What we miss so much in the West, those of us who come from the outlying regions, is perhaps that: that original nature where our identity bursts forth with theirs. The result is that the Most Royal Lady is right: their victory over us is also an accident. This feeling of exile which weighs upon us does not mean that we should be useless, but, on the contrary, establishes the necessity for us, and indicates our most urgent task, which is that of clearing the ground around nature. This task is ennobling."

Captain Hubert fidgeted in his chair.

"I confess that I don't understand," he said. "All this seems to me too—how shall I say it?—too much divorced from reality. The reality is that we have great need of them and they are at our disposal. Or we are at theirs, it doesn't much matter."

"You are mistaken, Captain: it matters a great deal."

He spoke in exasperation, but he felt ashamed of being so carried away, and he continued, more calmly:

"I understand your point of view very well, and in a sense I admit it. But excuse me for saying that it seems to me insufficient. You claim that the great need we have of the West leaves us no further choice, and merely authorizes submission, until the day when we shall have acquired mastery of them."

"Since you understand so well," said the captain, smiling, "will you explain to me why your generation does not accept the inevitable, and seems so badly to support that idea."

"It is because if we accept it and accommodate ourselves to it, we shall never have the mastery of the object. For we shall have no more dignity than it has. We shall not dominate it. Have you noticed that? It's the same gesture as that of the West, which masters the object and colonizes us at the same time. If we do not awake the West to the difference which separates us from the object, we shall be worth no more than it is, and we shall never master it. And our defeat will be the end of the last human being on this earth."

The bejeweled princess broke in noisily.

"You, you new Negroes, you are degenerates," she attacked them. "You do not know any more how to eat. You do not know any more how to pay attention to women. You spend your lives in frantic interminable debates. Now then, eat! When you have discovered again how to do that, you will have rediscovered everything."

Pierre-Louis, with roundabout manoeuvers, was trying to have Samba Diallo sit beside him at the table. The princess noticed this.

"Come here, young man," she called out. "You are to be between Adèle and me."

"How right you are, Madame," Samba Diallo said to her. "We are no longer living. We are empty of substance, and our head devours us. Our ancestors were more alive. Nothing separated them from themselves."

"Isn't that so?" the princess cried out in delight. "The men were full to bursting. They did not have any of your morose thoughts."

"That," declared Samba Diallo, "is because they had riches which we lose a little more every day. They had God. They had the family, which was only one single being. Within themselves they possessed the world. We are losing all that, little by little, in despair."

"I am indeed of your opinion, Samba Diallo," said Marc, fixing a touching gaze upon their visitor. "I am indeed of your opinion," he repeated thoughtfully, in a lower tone.

The captain burst out laughing, and Samba Diallo gave a start.

"And you, my little Adèle—you are also of their opinion, aren't you?" Captain Hubert demanded.

Adèle smiled confusedly, looked at Samba Diallo, then dropped her head without making any reply.

But the captain, abandoning his daughter, had turned toward Marc.

Samba Diallo was conscious that someone was speaking to him. It was Adèle, at whose left he had been seated. The girl had succeeded in conquering the overwhelming feeling of timidity which had paralyzed her in the presence of Samba Diallo ever since she had opened the door to him.

"I should like to say—" she began.

Samba Diallo encouraged her with a smile and leaned toward her, for she was speaking in a low tone, careful not to disturb the conversation going on among the men around her.

"I have never been in Africa, and I should so much like to go there," she said. "It seems to me that if I were there I should learn very quickly to 'understand' things as you do. They must be so much more true, seen like that."

"Perhaps that should not be, rightly," he answered. "It is to learn to 'understand' otherwise that we are here, all of us who are not of the West. It is for that that you ought to be born here."

"But that isn't what I want! Here, everything is so arid. You know, I understood very well, when you were talking just now. How right you were!"

Her big eyes were fixed on Samba Diallo, full of hope, as if she were expecting him to give her, immediately, that power of "understanding" things and people which he had evoked.

"Would she really feel 'exile'—this girl born on the banks of the Seine?" he was asking himself. "Yet she has never known any life but this. And her uncle Marc? At my first words they recognized themselves as belonging to us. The sun of their knowledge—can it truly be nothing to the darkness of our skin?"

Samba Diallo was far from suspecting the considerable effect which his words—those avowals which he had regretted as soon as he had uttered them—had produced on the girl who was "the exile on the banks of the Seine." Adèle's exile was in many respects even more dramatic than his own. He, at least, was a "half-breed" only by his culture. The West had become involved in his life insidiously, with the thoughts on which he had been nourished every day since the first morning when he had entered the foreign school in the town of L. The resistance of the Diallobé country had warned him of the risks of the Western adventure.

The ever-living example of his country was there, finally, to prove to him, in his moments of doubt, the reality of a non-Western universe. Adèle did not have her country of the Diallobé. When she happened to discern in herself a feeling or a thought which seemed to her to cut in a certain fashion into the backdrop of the Occident, her reaction for a long time had been to run away from it in terror, as from a monstrosity. Far from any diminution of this ambiguity, it was, on the contrary, accentuated, so that, progressively, Adèle yielded to the conviction that she was in some way abnormal. This evening, in speaking without restraint, as he had done, of what he himself was not far from considering as a shameful monstrosity, Samba Diallo came without knowing it to give a human visage to that part of her which the girl believed to be faceless.

6

"Adèle," Samba Diallo called.

"Yes."

"I believe that I hate them."

She took his arm and made him walk.

The autumn had ripened, and then stripped, the foliage of the trees. A sharp little wind was driving the strollers from the quays. Adèle pushed Samba Diallo toward the cross-walk. They crossed the street and made their way toward a café.

"I don't hate them as you perhaps think, as your grandfather does, for example. My hatred is more complicated. It is painful. It is from love repressed."

They went into an almost empty café and took a corner table.

"What would you wish us to serve you?"

The boy was waiting. They ordered two coffees, and remained silent until he came back. Having served them, he went away.

"My hatred is a re-inhibition, if I may use that word, an annulment, of love. I loved them too soon, unwisely, without knowing them well enough. Do you understand? They are of a strange nature. They do not inspire simple sentiments. No one should ally himself with them without having observed them well beforehand."

"Yes. But they do not leave time for that to the people whom they conquer."

"Then the people they conquer ought to remain on guard. They ought not to love them. The most poisoned hatreds are those born of old loves. Don't you hate them?"

"I don't know," she replied.

"I believe that you love them. It seems to me that at the very beginning one cannot not love them, in spite of what they do."

"Tell me how they conquered you, personally," she demanded.

She took advantage of the pause to leave the chair she was sitting in and settle herself next to Samba Diallo on the banquette.

"I don't know any too well. Perhaps it was with their alphabet. With it, they struck the first hard blow at the country of the Diallobé. I remained for a long time under the spell of those signs and those sounds which constitute the structure and the music of their language. When I learned to fit them together to form words, to fit the words together to give birth to speech, my happiness knew no further limit.

"As soon as I knew how to write, I began to flood my father with letters that I wrote to him and delivered to him with my own hand. This was to demonstrate my new knowledge and also, by keeping my gaze fixed on him while he was reading, to establish the fact that with my new tool I should be able to transmit my thought to him without opening my mouth. I had interrupted my studies with the teacher of the Diallobé at the very moment when he was about to initiate me at last into the rational understanding of what up to then I had done no more than recite—with wonder, to be sure. With these new skills I was suddenly entering, all on one floor, a universe which was, at the very first, one of marvellous comprehension and total communion. . . .

"As for the teacher of the Diallobé, he had taken his time. Wishing to teach his pupils God, he believed that he had his whole lifetime to do that.

"That is how it is, Adèle. But they—they interposed themselves, and undertook to transform me in their image. Progressively, they brought me out from the heart of things, and accustomed me to live at a distance from the world."

She snuggled closer against him.

"I hate them," she said.

Samba Diallo gave a start, and looked at her. She was leaning all the weight of her body against him, and her eyes, half-closed, were fixed on the street.

He was swept through by a strange disturbance. He gently pushed her away and, ceasing to snuggle against him, she raised her face toward his.

"You must not do that, Adèle," he said.

"Must not do what?"

"You must not hate them."

"Then you must teach me to penetrate to the heart of the world."

"I don't know whether one can ever find that road again, once one has lost it," he responded, in deep thought.

He felt that she was drawing away from him, and

he looked at her. She was weeping, silently, now. He took her hand, but she got up from the banquette.

"I must go home now," she said.

"I am going with you."

They left the café, and Samba Diallo hailed a taxi. When he had set Adèle down at her own door he made his way again, on foot, toward the subway.

It was there that, when the train had started, his memory suddenly brought a face before him. He saw it with an intensity that was almost hallucinating: there opposite him, in the yellow light and among the huddled crowd of passengers, had risen up the face of the teacher of the Diallobé. Samba Diallo closed his eyes, but the face never moved. In his thought he called to him:

"Master, what is left for me? The shadows are closing in on me. I no longer burn at the heart of people and things."

The teacher's face was unmoving. He was not laughing. He was not angry. He was grave and attentive. Samba Diallo invoked him anew:

"You who have never been distracted from the wisdom of the shadows, you who alone possess the Word, and have a voice sufficiently strong to rally and guide those who are lost, I implore the grace of your outcry in the darkness, the shout of your voice, to revive me to the secret tenderness—"

But the face was gone.

7

Samba Diallo received the knight's letter the next day:

"It is my opinion that you should return home. The fact that you will not have brought your studies to the end you would have wished is of little importance.

"It is high time that you should come back, to learn that God is not commensurable with anything, and especially not with history, whose vicissitudes are powerless in relation to His attributes. I know that the Occident, to which I have been so wrong as to send you, has a different faith on that score—a faith of which I recognize the utility, but which we do not share. Between God and man there exists not the slightest consanguinity, nor do I know what historic relationship. If there were, our recriminations would have been admissible. We should have been entitled to harbor resentment against Him for our tragedies, which would manifestly have revealed His imperfections. But this is not the case. God is not our parent. He is entirely outside the stream of flesh, blood, and history which links us together. We are free! See, now, why it seems to me unlawful to found the vindication on history, and senseless to rail against God by reason of our misery.

"These mistakes, nevertheless, whatever might be their intrinsic gravity, would not have troubled me beyond measure—so generalized are they—if at the same time you had not confessed to a more personal and more profound disquietude. You are afraid that God has abandoned you, because you no longer have the full sense of Him that you had in the past, and, as He has promised to His faithful ones, 'closer than the carotid artery.' So, you are not far from considering Him as having betrayed you.

"But you have not stopped to think that the traitor might be yourself. And yet— But answer rather: do you give God the entire place that is due Him, in your thoughts and in your actions? Do you insist upon putting your thoughts in conformity with His law? It is not a matter of paying allegiance to Him once for all, through a general and theoretical profession of faith. It has to do with your making yourself bring *every one* of your thoughts into conformity with the idea you grasp of His order and discipline. Are you doing that?

"I believed that I had talked with you enough about the merits of religious practice. The West, where you are now living, believes that God grants or withholds faith as it pleases Him. I will not debate this point of view, which I share. But I believe also that the omnipotence of God the Creator is such, rightly, that nothing would know how to gainsay it, not even the affirmation of our free determination. Your salvation, the presence of God living in you, depends upon yourself. You will obtain both these if, in mind and body, you rigorously observe His law, which religion has codified.

"But, precisely, it is there, when it is no longer a question of philosophizing, that strong minds stumble pitifully and run aground. And you who, from a vigorous thought, raise yourself to the understanding of God and claim to take Him in default, do you know only the road of the mosque? You will nail God to the pillory when you will have sought for Him, as He has said, and He will not have come. . . ."

8

"Master, it is the hour of prayer, let us go to the mosque," said the fool, catching hold of Samba Diallo by the chin, as if to force him to look at him.

"No, I am not the master," Samba Diallo responded. "Don't you see that I am not the master? The master is dead."

"Yes, master, let us go to the mosque."

Samba Diallo made a weary gesture.

"And, besides, I am not going to the mosque. I have already told you not to call me any longer to prayer."

"Yes, teacher of the Diallobé, you are right. You are tired. They are so tiring, aren't they? Rest now. When you have rested, we will go to the mosque. Isn't that so? Tell me, isn't that so?" he repeated, once more catching hold of Samba Diallo's chin.

His patience exhausted, Samba Diallo gave him a slight push.

It was enough to make the fool lose his balance, and he fell, rather grotesquely. Samba Diallo was seized by such pity, sweeping all through him, that he dropped to the ground, lifted the fool up, and pressed him to his breast.

The man broke into sobs, extricated himself from

Samba Diallo's embrace, looked at him with eyes full of tears, and said,

"You see, you are the teacher. . . . You are the teacher of the Diallobé. I am going to the mosque. I shall come back. Wait for me."

He turned his back and went away, with a light and springing step.

In spite of the frock-coat he was wrapped up in and the voluminous white boubous that he wore under it, one felt that his silhouette had grown less. The neck and the head, which emerged from the mass of his garments, were slender and pinched. From the little fellow's whole being there emanated a poignant tranquility and melancholy. He disappeared, now, behind the palisade.

For the fool, the teacher of the Diallobé was not dead, although he had been the most constant witness of the old man's last agonies, two months before.

One morning he had arrived at the house, long silent, of his friend. As he entered the teacher's room he had seen him praying as the dying pray. He was not rising: seated on his prayer rug, facing the east, he was merely sketching out the movements of the prayer, and had not the strength to complete them. The fool had remained at the door, fascinated by this broken prayer, this incongruous and tragic dumb show. He had waited there until the teacher had finished.

"You see," his friend, covered with perspiration and gasping, had said to him, "you see the extent to which God has showered His grace upon me. He has given me to live until the hour—of praying in this fashion—which He had foreseen from all eternity and set in His code. . . . You see—I have the strength. Look—Oh, look!"

And the teacher had recommenced his crippled prayer.

The fool had dashed outside and had run, without stopping, as far as the chief's house. He had found him in audience, and had stepped over the men seated there in quest of justice.

"I believe," he said, breathlessly, "that the teacher's hour has come."

The chief had bent his head and, slowly, pronounced the *chahâda* before getting up.

The fool, meanwhile, had gone away again. In the teacher's room he had found his family, together with Demba. Making his way through the company to the side of his friend, who lay stretched out on a mat, he had half lifted him and supported him against his breast. His tears were falling slowly on the perspiring face of the dying man.

"You see, He is there, my Friend is there," the weak voice was murmuring. "I well know that it was the great clamor of my life which hid Thee from me, Oh, my Creator. Now that the day is sinking, I see Thee. Thou art there."

The room was becoming completely filled. The new arrivals sat down in silence. Then the whole house became full of people, and people were sitting in the neighboring streets. They were running up from all sides. Soon the entire village was no more than an immense assemblage of men, seated there in silence.

"Master, take me with you, do not leave me here," the fool was whispering, as he cradled the dying man with a slow movement of his head and shoulders.

"My God, I thank Thee—for this grace which Thou hast bestowed upon me," the feeble voice went on, "to sustain me with Thy presence, to fill me with Thyself as Thou art doing now, even before I die."

"Hush. . . . Be still. Be still now, they are listening to you," and the fool placed a blunt hand across the dying man's mouth.

At the same time he looked around with tear-drenched eyes, as if to assure himself that no one had heard.

No person in the assemblage, not even the chief of the Diallobé, who was crouched close against the teacher and lost in prayer, would have dared to intervene to push the fool aside.

Suddenly the teacher stiffened, pronounced the name of God, and seemed slowly to relax. The fool laid him on the ground, left the room without a glance at anyone, and went out.

Then, outside, the great funeral *tabala** sounded. The silent village knew that the teacher had ceased to live.

No one saw the fool at the burial. He reappeared only on the following day, calm and once more serene, denying that the teacher was dead, yet refusing nevertheless to go to visit him at his house, as he had been doing every day.

When Samba Diallo came home, some little time

* Drum announcing important news.

after this, the fool postponed a call upon him until after the delegations from all parts of the country had gone away. He arrived alone, and found Samba Diallo reclining on a rattan couch in the courtyard of the chief's house, surrounded by members of his family. He paused some steps away, took a long look at the young man, whom he was seeing for the first time, then approached him and sat down on the ground.

"Teacher of the Diallobé, you have come back? That is good," the fool said.

There was laughter around them.

"But no, I am not the teacher of the Diallobé. I am Samba Diallo."

"No," said the fool. "You are the teacher of the Diallobé."

He kissed Samba Diallo's hand.

"Nothing can be done about it," said the chief, smiling.

Samba Diallo drew back his hand, which he had felt to be damp. He raised the fool's bent head, and saw that he was weeping.

"He has been like that since the teacher's death," said the chief. "He cries all the time."

Samba Diallo stroked the head of the little man seated on the ground.

"I have come from the country of the white men," he said to him. "It seems that you have been there. Then how was it?"

There was an impassioned gleam in the fool's eyes.

"Truly? You want me to tell you?"

"Yes, tell me."

"Master, they have no more bodies, they have no more flesh. They have been eaten up by objects. In order that they may move, their bodies are shod with large rapid objects. To nourish themselves, they put iron objects between their hands and their mouths. That is true!" he added, abruptly, turning with an aggressive air toward those present, as if he had been contradicted.

"It is indeed true," said Samba Diallo, thoughtfully. The fool, calmed, looked at him, smiling.

9

On the horizon, the setting sun had dyed the heavens with a tone of blood-stained purple. Not a breath of air stirred the motionless trees. The only sound to be heard was the great voice of the river, reverberating from its dizzily steep banks. Samba Diallo bent his gaze toward this voice, and saw the clay cliff in the distance. He remembered that in his childhood he had believed for a long time that this immense crevasse divided the universe into two parts, which were united by the river.

The fool, who was some distance ahead of him, retraced his steps, took him by the arm, and pulled him along.

Suddenly he realized where the fool was leading him. His heart began to beat fast. This was indeed the little road where his naked feet had been scratched, in the old days, by the thorns. Here was indeed the same ant-hill deserted by its inhabitants. At the turn of the road, this would be—this would be Old Rella and the City of the Dead.

Samba Diallo paused. The fool wanted to push him on and, not succeeding in this, let go of him and ran ahead by himself. Samba Diallo followed slowly. The fool passed Old Rella's renovated mausoleum, ran across the tombs, and abruptly crouched down close to one of them.

Samba Diallo stopped short, motionless. He saw that the fool was praying.

"You—you have not prayed," remarked the little fellow, panting.

It was the same tomb, the same orientation, the same little oblong heap of earth, as all the others about it. Nothing distinguished the mound where the teacher of the Diallobé lay from the other mounds all around.

Samba Diallo felt that a great lump was rising within him, that it was submerging him, moistening his eyes and his nostrils, making his mouth tremble. He turned around. The fool had just planted himself before him, and now took hold of his chin, violently.

"People are not obliged to pray. Do not tell me to pray, do not tell me any more, ever," Samba Diallo said.

The fool scrutinized the other man's face, then, slowly, smiled.

"Yes, teacher of the Diallobé. You are right. You are still tired. When you have rested from *their* fatigue, you will pray."

Samba Diallo's thought was an invocation:

"Teacher of the Diallobé, my master, I know that you have no longer a body of flesh and blood, that you no longer have eyes open in the darkness. I know, but thanks to you I am not afraid." His thought went on:

"I know that the earth has absorbed that miserable body which I used to see only a short time ago. I do not believe, as you had taught me when I was a child, that Azrael, the angel of death, would have cleaved through the earth beneath, to come in search of you. I do not believe that down there, underneath you, there is a great hole through which you have passed with your terrible companion. I do not believe—I do not believe very much any more, of what you had taught me. I do not know what I believe. But the extent is so vast, of what I do not know, and what I ought indeed to believe. . . ."

Samba Diallo sat down on the ground.

"How I wish that you might still be here, to oblige me to believe, and to tell me what! Your burning faggots on my body. . . . I remember and I understand. Your Friend, the One who has called you to Him does not offer Himself. He subdues Himself. At the price of pain. That I understand, again. That is perhaps why so many people, here and elsewhere, have fought and are dead, joyously. . . . Yes, perhaps at bottom that is it. . . . In dying amid the great clamor of battles waged in the name of your Friend, it is themselves whom all these fighters want to banish, so that they may be filled with Him. Perhaps, after all. . . ."

Samba Diallo felt that someone was shaking him. He raised his head.

"The shadows are falling. See, it is twilight. Let us pray," said the fool, gravely.

Samba Diallo made no response.

"Let us pray, Oh, let us pray," the fool implored. "If we do not pray immediately, the hour will pass, and neither of the two will be content."

"Who?"

"The teacher and his Friend. Let us pray, Oh, let us pray!"

He had seized Samba Diallo at the neck of his boubou, and was shaking him.

"Let us pray, speak, let us pray."

The veins of his face were standing out. His visage had become haggard.

Samba Diallo pushed him from him and got up to go away.

"You cannot go away like that, without praying!" the fool cried. "Stop, Oh stop! You cannot!"

"Perhaps, after all," Samba Diallo was thinking. "To constrain God. . . . To give Him the choice, between His return within your heart and your death, in the name of His glory."

"You cannot go away. Stop, Oh stop! Master—"

"He cannot evade the choice, if I constrain Him truly, from the bottom of my heart, with all I have of sincerity. . . ."

"Tell me that you will pray at last tomorrow, and I will leave you. . . ."

As he spoke, the fool had begun to walk along behind Samba Diallo, burrowing feverishly into the depths of his frock-coat.

"Thou wouldst not know how to forget me like that. I will not agree, alone for us two, to suffer from Thy withdrawal. I will not agree. No. . . ."

The fool was in front of him.

"Promise me that you will pray tomorrow."

"No—I do not agree. . . ."

Without noticing, he had spoken these words aloud.

It was then that the fool drew his weapon, and suddenly everything went black around Samba Diallo.

10

Quite close by, a voice spoke:

"My presence disturbs him now. Delicious welcome which the parched valley offers to the stream when it comes back. You are rejoicing in the stream."

"I was waiting for you. I have waited for a long time. I am ready."

"Are you at peace?"

"I am not at peace. I have waited for you for a long time."

"You know that I am the darkness."

"I have chosen. I have chosen you, my brother of darkness and of peace. I was waiting for you."

"The darkness is profound, but it is peace."

"I wish for it."

"Appearance and its reflections sparkle and crackle. Shall you not regret appearance and its reflections?"

"I wish for you."

"Say, you will regret nothing?"

"No. I am tired of this closed circle. My thought always returns upon myself, reflected by appearance, when, seized by disquiet, I have thrown it out like a tentacle."

"But it returns to you. Toward whatever side you turn, it is your own countenance that you see, nothing but that. You alone fill the closed circle. You are king. . . ."

"The mastery of the appearance is appearance."

"Then come. Forget, forget the reflection. Expand. You are spread and span. See how the appearance cracks and yields. See!"

"Farther, farther still!"

"Light and sound, form and light, all that is opposed and aggressive, blinding suns of exile, you are all forgotten dreams."

"Where are you? I no longer see you. There is only that turgescence which rises up in me, as the new water does in the river in flood."

"Be attentive. See what brings about the great reconciliation. The light stirs the darkness, love dissolves hate. . . ."

"Where are you? I hear nothing, save that echo in me which speaks when you have not finished speaking."

"Be attentive—for, see, you are reborn to being. There is no more light, there is no more weight, the darkness is no more. Feel how antagonisms do not exist."

"Farther away, still farther. . . ."

"Feel how thought no longer returns to you like a wounded bird, but is unfurled infinitely, no sooner have you dared it!"

"Wisdom, I sense your approach! Singular light of the depths, you are not circumventing, you are penetrating."

"Be attentive, for here is the truth: you are not that nothing which is confined by your senses. You are the infinite which scarcely holds back what your senses confine. No, you are not that closed disquiet which cries out in the midst of exile."

"I am two simultaneous voices. One draws back and the other increases. I am alone. The river is rising. I am in its overflow. . . . Where are you? Who are you?"

"You are entering the place where there is no ambiguity. Be attentive, for here, now, you are arriving. You are arriving."

"Hail! I have found again the taste of my mother's milk; my brother who has dwelt in the land of the shadows and of peace, I recognize you. Announcer of the end of exile, I salute you."

"I am bringing your kingdom back to you. Behold the moment, over which you reign. . . ."

"The moment is the bed of the river of my thought. The pulsations of the moments have the pulsations of thought; the breath of thought glides into the blowpipe of the moment. In the sea of time, the moment bears the image of the profile of man, like the reflection of the *kailcédrat* on the sparkling surface of the lagoon. In the fortress of the moment, man in truth is king, for his thought is all-powerful, when it is. Where it has passed, the pure azure crystallizes in forms. Life of the moment, life without age of the moment which endures, in the flight of your élan man creates himself indefinitely. At the heart of the moment, behold man as immortal, for the moment is infinite, when it is. The purity of the moment is made from the absence of time. Life of the moment, life without age of the moment which reigns, in the luminous arena of your duration man unfurls himself to infinity. The sea! Here is the sea! Hail to you, rediscovered wisdom, my victory! The limpidness of your wave is awaiting my gaze. I fix my eyes upon you, and you harden into Being. I am without limit. Sea, the limpidity of your wave is awaiting my gaze. I fix my eyes upon you, and you glitter, without limit. I wish for you, through all eternity."

THE AFRICAN WRITERS SERIES

The book you have been reading is part of Heinemann's
long-established series of African fiction. A list of the other titles
available in this series is given below, but for a catalogue giving
information on all the titles available in this series and in the Caribbean Writers
Series write to:

Heinemann Educational Publishers
Halley Court, Jordan Hill, Oxford OX2 8EJ
or e-mail: export.repp@repp.co.uk

United States customers should write to:
Heinemann Inc, 361 Hanover Street,
Portsmouth, NH 03801-3959, USA
or e-mail: custserv@heinemann.com

NOVELS

Mine Boy, Peter Abrahams
Wounding Words: A Woman's Journal in Tunisia, Evelyne Accad
Anthills of the Savannah, Chinua Achebe
Arrow of God, Chinua Achebe (not available in the USA, available in Kenya
through EAEP only)
Girls at War, Chinua Achebe (not available in the USA)
A Man of the People, Chinua Achebe (not available in the USA, available in
Kenya through EAEP only)
No Longer at Ease, Chinua Achebe (available in Kenya through EAEP only)
Things Fall Apart, Chinua Achebe.
The Trouble with Nigeria, Chinua Achebe
The Heinemann Book of Contemporary African Short Stories, Chinua Achebe
and C L Innes (eds)
African Short Stories, Chinua Achebe and C L Innes (eds)
The Concubine, Elechi Amadi
The Great Ponds, Elechi Amadi
The Beautyful Ones Are Not Yet Born, Ayi Kwei Armah
Fragments, Ayi Kwei Armah (not available in the USA)
The Healers, Ayi Kwei Armah (not available in the USA)
Two Thousand Seasons, Ayi Kwei Armah (not available in the USA)
So Long a Letter, Mariama Bâ
The Sympathetic Undertaker and Other Dreams, Biyi Bandele-Thomas
The Origin of Life and Death, Ulli Beier (ed)
Mission to Kala, Mongo Beti
The Poor Christ of Bomba, Mongo Beti
Loukoum: The Little Prince of Belleville, Calixthe Beyala
The Sun Hath Looked Upon Me, Calixthe Beyala
Your Name Shall Be Tanga, Calixthe Beyala
I Write What I Like, Steve Biko (not available in the USA)
A Duty of Memory, WPB Botha
Wantok, WPB Botha
The Heinemann Book of African Women's Writing, Charlotte Bruner (ed)

Striving for the Wind, Meja Mwangi
Devil on the Cross, Ngũgĩ wa Thiong'o
Detained: A Writer's Prison Diary, Ngũgĩ wa Thiong'o
A Grain of Wheat, Ngũgĩ wa Thiong'o (available in Kenya through EAEP only)
Matigari, Ngũgĩ wa Thiong'o (not available in the USA)
Petals of Blood, Ngũgĩ wa Thiong'o (not available in the USA, available in
Kenya through EAEP only)
The River Between, Ngũgĩ wa Thiong'o (available in Kenya through EAEP only)
Secret Lives, Ngũgĩ wa Thiong'o (available in Kenya through EAEP only)
Weep Not, Child, Ngũgĩ wa Thiong'o (available in Kenya through EAEP only)
Efuru, Flora Nwapa
The Voice, Gabriel Okara
God's Bits of Wood, Sembène Ousmane
The Last of the Empire, Sembène Ousmane
The Money Order with White Genesis, Sembène Ousmane
Xala, Sembène Ousmane
Hare and Hornbill, Okot p'Bitek
Houseboy, Ferdinand Oyono
The Old Man and the Medal, Ferdinand Oyono
Mayombe, Pepetela
Yaka, Pepetela
Hill of Fools, R L Peteni
Mhudi, Sol T Plaatje
Distant View of a Minaret, Alifa Rifaat
Season of Migration to the North, Tayeb Salih
Jesus is Indian and Other South African Stories, Agnes Sam
On Trial for My Country, Stanlake Samkange
The Narrow Path, Francis Selormey
Colour Me Blue, Gaele Sobott-Mogwe
The Interpreters, Wole Soyinka
The Seven Solitudes of Lorsa Lopez, Sony Labou Tansi
The Case of the Socialist Witchdoctor and Other Stories, Hama Tuma
The Gunny Sack, M G Vassanji
Smouldering Charcoal, Tiyambe Zeleza

POETRY
A Simple Lust, Dennis Brutus
The Heinemann Book of African Women's Poetry, Frank and Stella Chipasula
(eds)
The Heinemann Book of African Poetry in English, Adewale Maja-Pearce (ed)
Of Chameleons and Gods, Jack Mapanje
The Chattering Wagtails of Mikuyu Prison, Jack Mapanje
Song of Lawino & Song of Ocol, Okot p'Bitek
Poems of Black Africa, Wole Soyinka (not available in the USA)

PLAYS
The Imprisonment of Obatala, Obotunde Ijimere
The Black Hermit, Ngũgĩ wa Thiong'o (available in Kenya through EAEP only)
The Trial of Dedan Kimathi, Ngũgĩ wa Thiong'o and Micere Mugo
I Will Marry When I Want, Ngũgĩ wa Thiong'o and Ngũgĩ wa Mirii